Re Verse

Re Verse

Essays on Poetry and Poets

David R. Slavitt

NORTHWESTERN UNIVERSITY PRESS
EVANSTON, ILLINOIS

Northwestern University Press
Evanston, Illinois 60208-4170

Printed in Canada

10 9 8 7 6 5 4 3 2 1

ISBN 0-8101-2084-4

Some of these essays have appeared in *Sewanee Review, Hudson Review, Harvard Review, Denver Quarterly, Boulevard, Hollins Critic, Southern Review,* and *Journal of Palliative Medicine.* The author is grateful to the editors of those publications.

Grateful acknowledgment is also made to the poets whose work I have reprinted here, their publishers, and the holders of their copyrights for permission to quote from various collections: Louisiana State University Press and Fred Chappell for "Message" from *Source* (1985) by Fred Chappell; the estate of Merrill Moore for poems from *Clinical Sonnets* (1949); the Department of English of the University of Missouri for poems from *I'll Be Home Late Tonight* (1967) and *The Tempo Changes. The Lights Go Up. The Partners Change* (1978) by Thomas McAfee; New Directions Publishing Corporation for poems by Dudley Fitts from *Poems, 1929–1936* (1937); Simon and Schuster, Inc., for "The Gardener" from *By Daylight and in Dream: New and Collected Poems, 1904–1970* (1970) by John Hall Wheelock; and the estate of Winfield Townley Scott for poems from *Collected Poems, 1937–1962.*

The author is also grateful to *Newsweek* for permission to quote the piece he wrote for that magazine about John Hall Wheelock, published in 1959.

Library of Congress Cataloging-in-Publication data are available from the Library of Congress.

♾ The paper used in this publication meets the minimum requirements of the American National Standard for Information Sciences—Permanence of Paper for Printed Library Materials, ANSI Z39.48-1992.

For the Pléiade

CONTENTS

Re Verse

A Master's Essay:
Dudley Fitts

A QUARTER CENTURY AGO, I wrote in a spiral notebook: "The gesture of picking up a fountain pen, unscrewing the cap, grasping the barrel, and preparing to write is not only sensuous and pleasurable, but, like all significant rituals, carries the promise of further satisfactions. No matter how disordered my life, no matter how low my spirits may be, there is always this refuge, the belief in the possibility that by this exercise I may reassert some kind of control upon the welter of experience, or at least impose some order upon my own perceptions and reactions. The fountain pen is one of those wonderful tools that molds itself to the hand, becoming an extension of the body of the craftsman. The look of a holograph page, moreover, bears the unmistakable stamp of one's own personality. By means of these idiosyncratic lines, recognizably my own, I can hope to tame the savage meaninglessness of the world and make it conform to my mind and hand in the way the gold tip of the pen has conformed itself, the resulting scratchless flow being, in all senses, the point toward which the art aspires.

"Still, the question cannot be answered so simply and neatly. I have been writing long enough now so that certain sophomoric problems pose themselves in a politely professional guise. The decisions one makes about style, tone, attack, and shape may seem to be technical, but, of course, they are always more than that. Lurking behind such craftsmanly choices are the real issues—for whom am I writing, and, more particularly, for whom am I writing *this*? With poetry, with fiction, one can assume an audience, however select or broad, however clever or dull, imagine a group of people, and leave to the rich diversity of creation the probability that such a group will exist. One can strike an aristocratic posture—as Mr. Nabokov has done, saying, 'I write for myself, my wife, and a few friends.' I have used his line myself, sometimes. With an autobiographical essay, however, such a reply is an evasion, for I have never dared to assume that even my friends are interested in *me*. I have been a performer, I think, in order to attract and beguile acquaintances into friendship and to appease friends into continuing their toleration of a personality I might not put up with myself if I were not condemned to it. My fear, then, in undertaking this exploration of my own life is that its proper audience may be a purely imaginary one and my fundamental fiction.

"Small children—especially eldest children, and I was one—have imaginary playmates in whose company they conspire against loneliness and boredom. Some such figure has persisted for me. My imaginary playmate is now my imaginary audience, nameless, featureless, but, like all such projections, concerned, sympathetic, cultivated in his tastes, demanding but forgiving, witty, well read, and above all a fan. The kind of understanding that identical twins are supposed to have for each other, we have. I write and he reads; I speak and he listens; but we think in unison, so that his objections, his questions are mine, just as, on good days, his approbation and delight are my own.

"For such loyal, understanding, discriminating attention, there is no one in the real world to whom I can turn with any confidence. I am forty years old, have a wife, three children, a sister, two living parents, friends, agents, editors, readers, and yet, unscrewing the cap of the fountain pen and positioning the spiral note-book at its usual angle on the black desk pad, I am alone each morning with that imaginary familiar, thrown back on the most primitive resources which, however inefficient and even absurd they may be, are those to which we always return, not necessarily because they work well, or even at all, but because they are the ones we know. In the course of time, we contrive refinements, and I have objectified my friendly phantom, turning him into the satisfaction I can take from the coils of syntax and the rhythms of a sentence. But it is his satisfaction and his pleasure, still.

"I have never been entirely comfortable about my relationship to my talent. Either I have identified myself with it, becoming in the process a mind on an uninteresting stalk, or I have separated from it, as Faulkner did, who thought of himself as the 'worthless husk' of his works—and this when he had received word of his having won the Nobel Prize.

"The only circumstance in which I can feel any real connection with my literary abilities is one in which I am depressed, afraid, and alone, and in which I sit down for the consoling and reassuring experience of putting words to paper, bringing to life that old friend who listens and reads, and taking solace in his company. Indeed, my impulse here is not, strictly speaking, autobiographical. Instead, what I'd rather do is to describe in some way the life and times of this non-existent but persistent friend, this fictive twin, whose tastes have changed, whose whims I have learned to intuit, and whose predilections it is my constant effort to please. A biography of a figment is a curious undertaking, no doubt, but all writing is curious, and the conformations required of the lives of writers to this arduous undertaking are most curious indeed. It makes a kind of comparative sense for me to address this alter ego directly, for if he is my reader, I may assume he is interested in reading about himself. Which of us is not?"

That old notebook turned up, as these things will, when I was hunting for something else in my study. A different room, a different life, a different wife, and a different self, too, I expect. But there are recognizable traits, if only in the hints of depression and the proclivity to hypotaxis. The imaginary reader is still with me, and I know him better now than I did, but even then I could see that much of him came from my connection with Dudley Fitts, who had been my teacher at Andover in my senior year and about whom I wrote my master's essay at Columbia five years later, in 1957. Indeed, those foregoing paragraphs were part of an introduction to a palimpsest I'd planned, a revision and improvement of that essay I had been carrying around for twenty years and still have now.

If both pieces, the twenty-two-year-old's and the forty-year-old's, seem arrogant now and rather unforgiving, I can see the worry that prompted those harsh responses. I was sure that Fitts's failure to keep on writing poetry after his first slender but impressive volume, *Poems, 1929–1936,* was a defeat. It may have been, but it now strikes me that his silence was his business and that my fears about my own prospects ought not have been projected in that way. The master's essay would have been much better if I had been content to read his poems rather than try to diagnose them or their author, for Fitts enabled as much as he frightened me.

Paradoxically, the forty-year-old's jottings could have been improved, too, if their author had been less condescending to his younger self. "I was frightened by Dudley Fitts' defeat," the notebook says, "because I had never before seen such impressive talent, such wit, such erudition muscle bound into impotence." In an unexamined way, I suppose I must have believed that all you had to do was have the talent, and maybe a little common sense, and you would eventually go on to succeed in writing or painting or composing or whatever it was. After all, all the biographies I read as a small boy worked out to nothing less than grandeur, even if posthumous. It never occurred to me that there is no great call for juvenile books on the lives of distinguished failures. And even if there had been such a series of volumes, I cannot think they would have had a place on the shelves in the children's room of the White Plains Public Library. The whole point of White Plains was its security, its determined pleasantness, its isolation from the metropolis to the south from which my parents had managed to escape and to which they returned only reluctantly, even to midtown, to shop or go to the theater. There is a point, driving north, where the parkway crosses the line that separates the Bronx from Westchester, and my father would always breathe a deep sigh of relief, as though he had been holding his breath for the five or six hours of our venture into what was obviously a bad place."

Fitts was, of course, a father figure, as masters are likely to be. He was the first published poet I had ever known, an aggressively intellectual man in an unintellectual, even anti-intellectual place. For a youngish, undersized, brainy guy like me to find a grown-up whose intellectual accomplishments were enough to get him excused from the coaching duties that were required of most of the rest of the Phillips Academy faculty and who inspired awe among his colleagues was a revelation to me: his very existence on that uncongenial and even hostile campus offered a glimpse of how I, too, might find acceptance and even success, there and later on in the wider world I already suspected might be no easier or more welcoming.

The year I studied with him, from 1951 to 1952, he was in his late forties. He died in 1969, at sixty-six, which is roughly my age now. But when I think of him, I am a teenager, impressed, even intimidated, by a man who was two years older than my father and, like my father, could modulate instantly from the serious to the playful. He could be witty, but the wit could be sharp. All his students were in awe of him, as I was, despite the fact that he was extraordinarily kind to me and very patient. I would appear every few weeks at his house in Hidden Field with a sheaf of poems the thickness of which would now represent a year's work, and he would give me tea and go over my efforts, line by line, explaining why this didn't work or why that was hopeless. And now and then, there'd be a line, or even two, with which there was nothing wrong, and he'd point that out, too, because the first thing a young writer needs to learn is how to read and how to distinguish what is good from what isn't. You can't fix a poem if you don't know what's wrong with it, or where it has gone squashy or bad.

Fitts was a hard taskmaster, but I welcomed that because it meant that he was taking me seriously. What I didn't realize at the time, at Andover, at Columbia, or even when I was writing in the notebook and going back over the old ground of my master's essay was how hard he was on himself. I do remember having lunch once with

Robert Fitzgerald, Fitts's former student and then collaborator and friend, whom I had sought out for information and another view of him. Fitzgerald was most genial and as a part of our greeting said that, because we had both studied under Dudley, that made us, in a way, brothers. From what he told me, what remains most vividly in my mind is his account of how, at Choate, where Fitts had taught English before coming to Andover and had also been the school organist, Fitzgerald had once sneaked into the chapel to listen to Fitts practicing. Whenever Fitts made a mistake, he'd swear at the organ and himself in a strenuous rage that was all the more impressive because of the setting. I later learned from Dana Gioia, who studied with Fitzgerald at Harvard, that Fitzgerald's grading system was more or less taken from Dudley's, and that he rated papers PB (pretty bad), NTB (not too bad), NB (not bad), and NAAB (not at all bad). "Good" was not a possible category.

With such hints as these—or, actually, billboards—I ought to have been able to summon up a little more generosity and sympathy for Fitts's poetic silence but, as I have suggested, my own fear prevented me from doing so. I was going through a bad patch, no longer able to make a living writing potboilers, but in bad enough odor with the intellectual establishment so that teaching jobs were not forthcoming. It is not surprising that I should have gone back to an old manuscript to try to get in touch with that optimism and even brashness that seemed at that moment so distant.

Fitts had died in 1969, and I thought it might be a reasonable thing to revisit that old essay of mine and perhaps even use it as an introduction for some kind of collection of Fitts's writings that I might try to get New Directions to publish. James Laughlin, the poet and the proprietor of that house, had been one of Fitts's Choate students.

If the 1957 essay seems stiff, that is partly because it was very much in the voice of academic writing of that time. I remember dictating the words into a secondhand Dictaphone machine with those peculiar wax cylinders, both to help get through the project and also to try to make it as conversational in tone as possible. I then did the transcription myself, editing as I went along. And when I was done, I turned it in to Richard W. B. Lewis and sent a copy to Fitts. The judgments it offered could not have been pleasing to the essay's subject: "The referential technique that pervades the poetry . . . is another part of this 'new writing,' for by implication it equates literature, words, and language with what might be called primary experience. There is no longer the distinction between the world of fact and event and the world of letters, for the two have been inextricably fused. The references and images that derive from language are countless. In Fitts's poetry we find, flipping the pages in a random fashion:

Yet you have said *I love I love* and broken
Your lips upon the words your lips have spoken

Our stammering dies
Ultimately, mine in you, and yours in me . . .

You then: the fixed metonymy of my being

      what remains now
but a mouthful of ashes, but words, but a girl's crying

Then he of his own death aware
Hears terribly at false dawn his own
Dead giggle, bursting from twisted
Lips, extinguish all the stars.

"Some of this we are prepared to accept. The tradition of eclectic writing, and the more than usual interest in language that has been displayed by the major poets of our time have helped us to grow accustomed to many of the technical devices that Dudley Fitts employed. Still, we cannot accept it all. Much of his poetry seems silly, even trivial—mere fun with words. We object to it because it is private fun, inaccessible not only to the common reader but even to the reader with a great fund of information—if that fund happens to differ from that of the poet.

"At first blush, Fitts' poetry seems to have no message; it seems to be sheer technique, and, although we have seen that the technique *is* the message, here, now, in 1957, that message is dated because the technique has largely been accepted into the current poetics. What was all experiment then is now either commonplace or demonstrably absurd.

"Fitts, having gone as far as he did, found suddenly that he could not go back. He had committed himself to a certain technique, to a certain way of thinking and writing. Finally he tired of the aesthete's pose, which is necessary for one who is to write in such a manner, and he retreated not merely from 'extreme' poetry, but from poetry altogether. He was convinced, finally, that there was more to poetry than rhetorical facade, and was convinced, too, that he was a rhetorician, pure and simple. He devoted himself, then, to translation, which is essentially a rhetorician's task. His career seems perfectly logical, if a little wasteful. It seems disappointing, for what Johnson said of Lyttleton can just as easily be said about Fitts: he 'shows a mind attentive to life and a power of poetry which cultivation might have raised to excellence.'"

It makes me cringe a little, even though, in a rough way, it is true enough. I wish the kid would shut up, stop pontificating, and just pay attention to the poems. Or, better yet, just to the good ones. There are plenty of bad poems in the world, and poets weed out the worst, or try to. What is left is what goes into the collection, and, unless there have been an extraordinarily fortunate series of encounters, the resulting book is generally a record of a few successes and then a number of less spectacular but—at least one hopes—competent performances that may somehow speak to some reader.

The poem that seems to have resonated most with me is "The Liturgy of Small Susan," which bears the epigraph:

> *And seyde, O deere child, I halse thee,*
> *In vertu of the Hooly Trinitee,*
> *Tell me what is thy cause for to synge,*
> *Sith that thy throte is kut, to my semynge?*

What the essay says is:

"The epigraph, of course, is from the 'Prioresse's Tale,' the 'deere child' being little Hugh of Lincoln, the subject of that tale of the miraculum, the dead child who still lives and sings. The death of the little girl is not told, but actually dramatized by pure grammar:

> Small Susan, clutching at Azraël's lapel—
> She died rapidly. We felt
> Sorry in unison. . . .

"The action in the participle, with Susan clutching, shows her to be alive and active, if unwell. She dies in the dash at the end of the line, so that there is reason for the hush of the simple 'She died rapidly,' and the even prissy decorum of 'We felt sorry in unison.' This is the composition of place. This is the action, the given, and the starting point of the poem.

"From here on, the speaker is engaged in an attempt to come to terms with the death, or, at least to arrive at a point of view. Despite the word 'unison,' there is no unified 'We' and, unlike the speaker of Ransom's 'Bells for John Whiteside's Daughter,' the speaker of 'Liturgy' is isolated, and, more important, unable to accept any of the traditional modes of response.

"There is an 'I' in this poem, (as there is not, in Ransom's) and the speaker here is not merely an observer, but a participant, and ultimately, the agonist.

> Small Susan, clutching at Azraël's lapel—
> She died rapidly. We felt
> Sorry in unison. The gent with the beard
> Precisely dropped a lovely tear;
> Mother crossed herself, and Pa
> Staggered down the stairs to crank the car.
>   ℣ It was very affecting.
>   ℟ We were moved, all of us.

"The 'gent with the beard,' who is a major figure of the poem, is related to the old man who appears so often in all the poetry." (The essay finally suggests that these elderly gentlemen may have something to do with Henry Fitts, Dudley's grandfather, who fought at Shiloh; returned to Haverhill, Massachusetts; and then, for the rest of his life, lived mostly in the attic and read Shakespeare. Dudley must have grown up feeling both pride and shame with this impressive half-mad grandfather upstairs. He kept Henry Fitts's saber on his desk in his study at Andover.)

"The specific term 'the beard' (as he is later called in the poem) is, Fitts tells me, acolyte slang (or anyway Anglican Acolyte, Boston, circa 1910) for God. I do not think that we are to take the gent as God himself—but there is probably the same kind of obscure relation or, anyway, association with divinity as we found in 'Preraphaelite Encounter,' where the girl calls her grandfather 'this peculiar Beatrice.' Here, he 'precisely dropped a lovely tear,' and we are left to puzzle out what that could mean.

"The phrase, of course, is applied by the speaker, himself *engagé*, and is therefore ambiguous. We do not know whether this is the actual manner and spirit of the gent's reaction, or whether the gent simply shed a tear (showed grief without positively bawling about it) and the adjectives 'precise' and 'lovely' were supplied by the outraged speaker. This latter possibility is certainly psychologically plausible. Here is this young man (younger, anyway, than the beard), beside himself with grief and therefore resenting the elder man's self-control that makes possible the traditional outward reaction. This reaction, impossible to the speaker, is characterized as being 'precise' and 'lovely' because, feeling great grief, and finding the proper response impossible, the speaker is inclined to believe that the 'beard's' behavior is artificial, and, therefore, insincere. At any rate, there is a kind of coldness implied by the manner in which the sentence is cast.

"Mother's actions are reported very flatly and Pa's behavior is treated with a certain patronizing tone by the bathetic ending of the line and stanza 'to crank the car.' Thus, the speaker finds it impossible to take his cue from any of the others. The father is slightly absurd, the mother's religiosity is inaccessible, and the gentle reaction, too, is inaccessible, but for another reason. There is, then, no small irony in the response: 'We were moved, all of us.'

"The second stanza is an exploration and an exhaustion of the possibilities for solace in literature. Plainly, the presence, the wisdom—or whatever it is that one must have to look upon death—cannot be derived from mere poetry:

> Death like a darling mannered cat
> Sedately pounced on Susan's back.
> Death is cleanlier at sea:
> Susan's hue is sub-marine.
> Death is handsomer in books:
> How natural small Susan looks!
>   ℣ Will you take lemon or an onion?
>   ℟ Profoundly.

"These are the formulations we find in poetry, and, lovely though they are, they are mainly irrelevant to the actual event of death. 'Full fathom five,' and all that, but here lies Susan, in the casket, looking almost as she did in sleep. There is a unique, terrible quality of the grotesque, which attends the mortician's art. Plainly, death is handsomer in books, and thus the verse's, 'Will you take lemon or an onion?'—the martini party question, which misses the mark 'Profoundly.'

"The speaker is incapable of formulating either the proper—or indeed any—consistent attitude about the decease of Susan, and, inasmuch as he has observed the various reactions of Ma, Pa, and the gent, it is natural that he should wonder which of them will assume those duties necessary for the required practical—as well as the emotional—farewell to the dead.

> Who shall weave her seamless shroud?
> Who depart the crape around?
> Who shall toll a careful knell?
> Who shall delve her house? who shall
> Pale her down lest the vampire come?
> 'Done,' quoth the beard; and it was done.
>   ℣ Some of them are my very best friends.
>   ℟ Did you have an easy decease?

"The central and active position, then, of the beard is affirmed, and then emphasized by the contrast with the personae involved in the versicle and response, who have here assumed roles not unlike those of the choragos and chorus of Greek tragedy.

"In the following stanza, the speaker's emotion mounts in pitch and intensity as his words become more and more stilted and his diction takes on a wrenched and peevish quality. It is, after all, the beard who bids farewell to Susan. He of the precise and lovely tear is the lay priest, whether the speaker likes it or not.

> Who'll troll a stave for her epicede?
> Who'll versify Small Susan's threne?
> Who'll thole her tholing? Who'll compound
> Her meed in strophic trentals loud?
> Who'll cheat the lyre of a deathsong?
> 'Sung,' quoth the beard; and it was sung;
> ℣ I sometimes think it's best we don't know.
> ℟ Did you speak?

"Of course, on the sheer narrative level, what has 'really' happened in these two stanzas is that the beard (probably, that is, the grandfather) has picked up the phone and called the undertaker, picked out the kind of funeral, selected the casket, and finally, chosen the hymn to be sung in church. To the speaker, however, these simple actions are endowed with a mystic nimbus of meanings.

"The song, which follows in the next three stanzas, repeats the figure presented in the opening stanza of the poem. Where, before, the mother, father, gent with beard, and speaker were isolated by their differing reactions, here, in a general way, several of the great cultural responses to death are presented and distinguished. These are not to be identified with the personae of the opening stanza, however, for the action of the song takes place within the mind of the speaker, each response figuring in that arena and going its own way, as analogue to the appearance and divergence of the people in the house. In the external world, it was the lack of community, the want of any consistent and homogeneous response that the speaker felt so keenly. Now, it is his own confusion and the contradictory impulses that he feels within himself that are disturbing. He moves from a bitter materialism, to a classic mythic consciousness, and then to a kind of low-grade, lyric Christianity, which has neither the simple, instinctive belief of Ma, nor the more sophisticated faith of which the refined speaker feels so much in need in these demanding times.

'Small Susan died last night. O loss
'Irreparable at any cost!
'Smiling she died, and, dead, she smiles
'In diminishing fragments. Crisply filed
'Away with worms, her corruptible clay
'Enriches our lawns till the Judgment Day.'
    ℣ We all come to it, sooner or later.
    ℟ She stains the time past, lights the time to come.

'What songs the Sirens sang, What name
'Achilles bore, What fretted place
'Trist Orpheus calmed, What harboring
'Orestes found at last, What wind
'Streaks thin the wail of damned wights:
'She knows, and, knowing, comfort finds.'
    ℣ I tore her tattered ensign down
    ℟ It was married chastity.

'Small Susan died. Who mourn for her,
'Commit her name to the plangent air.
'Bespeak the ouzel and the wren,
'The halcyon and ptarmigan:
'These the undersong divide,
'And shrill her planh along the sky.'
    ℣ One can be too careful.
    ℟ And one clear call for me.

"Here, in the speaker's mind, the theme of literature returns, as, throughout, words and phrases echo the speaker's reading. They are applied, however, with an ironic twist. In the first stanza of the song, the discussion of the material decomposition of her body is worked through Webster's great line from *The Duchess of Malfi*, but here, the line is intended literally. 'She stains the time past'—decomposes, becomes part of a tree, a piece of coal, or peat, even, and 'lights the time to come.' The verse and response of the following stanza are partly playful, too. The allusion is to Oliver W. Holmes's more or less corny first line in 'Old Ironsides': 'Aye, tear her tattered ensign down.' The response (from the threnos of 'The Phoenix and the Turtle,' of Shakespeare) is a kind of barely relevant spiritualism.

"The third stanza is the most difficult one to understand, mainly because of its highly specialized references. These are not ordinary birds, but particular, symbolic ones. The difficulty does not stem from the symbolism, but from the fact that the symbolism is the central image. The sensibility here invoked is that of religious feeling reduced to the pastoral level, which Fitts identified with the Provençal lyric. ('Planh' is a Provençal word meaning 'plaint,' or 'complaint,' which Pound has used on occasion.) The Provençal mind, which fused pastoral literature and religion to produce its very special kind of poetry, is plainly relevant to the speaker's quandary, and it is invoked here as a wrong answer, undercut immediately (the response is from Tennyson's 'Crossing the Bar') and replaced later by something else. It stands, however, as a progress report as of the beginning of the mass.

"The narrative continues as the speaker presents his impressions of the requiem:

> The Altarboy gapes adenoids, and
> Father Considine can't bend
> Downward from the loins, or up-
> Ward from the loins: the Mass is a gyp,
> The broad is leaven! the chalice dusty!
> She rests in peace, gents; don't be fussy.
>   ℣ I'm sure it was the better way.
>   ℟ All we like sheep.
>
> The beard is wet, and wags amain.
> Father Considine displays
> Fulgid the theophagic host.

Mass is said. Her soul's at rest.
Gentles, your prayers to ease the way:
Small Susan shinnies Peter's gate.
     ℣ An arcane smile dilutes my countenance.
     ℟ A novel situation this.

"What begins as pure spleen is somehow altered here. The bitterness of the response, 'All we like sheep,' wrenched from Isaiah, and
the slangy 'She rests in peace, gents;' changes abruptly after 'Mass
is said.' Suddenly the gent, who has been a foil to the speaker
throughout, and who has generalized here to include all the assembled celebrants, is transformed by the shift from 'gents' to 'gentles.'

"The Mass has effected a conciliation for the speaker, not with
death, but with the others (the gentles), thus leaving the speaker isolated in his bereavement. He is not cut off from the others, as he was
previously; but now as he accepts them, they do not impinge upon his
consciousness and he is alone with Susan, who, in his imagination,
can, indeed, shinny Peter's gate.

"In this isolation, the literary sensibility again comes to the fore.
For the first time, it has come into its own, and the speaker's use of
letters demonstrates this. The quotations are not used to undercut
other attitudes by their misapplication, nor are they used to undercut
the literary sensibility itself, by their inherent triteness.

"The poem concludes:

O carefull Verse! her light is gutted—
(Acridly, teeth on edge, prevent her)
O heavie Herse! her path's be-nighted—
(Portal of lead: and enter, enter,
All my love!)—Sweet whoreson Death,
Ev'n now I top her in your bed!
     ℣ The street is dark, I shall stumble.
     ℟ Sirs, in my heart there was a kind of fighting.

"It is no longer the Provençal lyric, but the Elizabethan that is now
appropriate. This is suggested by the specialized historical use of

'herse' (meaning a framework over a tomb to support rich coverings and palls) and insisted upon by the archaic spelling. 'Sweet whoreson Death' is also used with the jocular familiarity the words carried in Elizabethan taverns, and it suggests the intimacy even beyond loathing that the speaker now feels. He is confused and uncertain, of course, but his confusion here is an ultimate one, and stems from the insoluble puzzle of mortality. The poem is resolved, however, for the speaker has managed to confront that puzzle with all he knows and with all he is. This is as much as anyone can do. The versicle and the response are allusive, still, but they support the stanza, and confirm its attitudes, which are by no means complacent.

"The versicle echoes Boyet's line in *Love's Labour's Lost,* 'A light for Monsieur Judas! It grows dark, he may stumble'; the response, of course, echoes Hamlet's.

"It would be too simple to say that the confusion had finally become an affirmative one. It would certainly be a distortion. However, it seems clear that the speaker has attained a kind of wholeness. The restraint of the last stanza, in regard to both the explicit emotion and the diction of the poetry, suggests that there is not so much of a gulf between the speaker and the gent with the beard as there had been before. Certainly, he is closer to Small Susan."

Mostly, I am depressed by my excessive reliance on the passive voice, my reckless disregard for the difference between "which" and "that" (which I have silently corrected), and my failure to point out what seems so clear now—that these are Eliot's techniques that were modish then ("The Wasteland" had been published when Fitts was an undergraduate at Harvard) but that had been abandoned in the fifties, by which time even Eliot had progressed to the later style of the "Four Quartets." I probably should have glossed "epicede," the Anglican form of "epicedium," a funeral ode. And I should have connected the uneasiness of the speaker to Fitts's own guardedness about any simple feeling, which may be commonplace and even trite but which nonetheless remains the currency of our large emotions. His speaker is so worried about risking inauthenticity or banality that he can hardly allow himself to feel at all.

My analysis of the reason for Fitts's silence now seems to me too theoretical and too much involved with the rise and decline of literary fashions and the demands that this may have put upon him to adapt and change. I think, now, that it was much simpler, a question mostly of his having raised his critical standards to such an exquisite level that he'd intimidated himself, could never be satisfied, and, more important and painful, could not risk direct statement of any kind. He wrote in my copy of *Poems, 1929–1936:* "This deplorable book of poems is inscribed to David Slavitt by Dudley Fitts, 11 Xber, 1951," which was not only excessively modest but also a preemptive closeout, anticipating any objection I might ever make. (When Fitzgerald inscribed my copy of their translation of *Oedipus Rex,* which Fitts, years before, had signed at the top of the page, he put his name down at the very bottom.)

No one can quarrel with high standards. But one can ask about how high they should be and at what cost they should be maintained. Elsewhere in the master's essay, I have a brief discussion of "Couplets for the Thirtieth Year," which is a relatively straightforward piece in tetrameter couplets that sound a little like Frost's or even Andrew Marvell's. It was a quirky gesture back then to do rhymed couplets in a poem not intended to be funny, but Fitts managed them quite well. The last part of the poem is:

> Play then: play men and women, all
> old shadows wavering on the wall;
> the days and nights of love and hate,
> and those whose friendship stayed too late;
> play kindliness that a word betrayed,
> and lust by a careful smile dismayed,
> play bedtime kiss and drowsy head,
> play all lost lovers, play the dead.
>
> And this be all your music, lest
> God know our last song for the best,
> and, hurrying down, the laggard night
> shroud shining song and singer bright.
> For, were we true in love and time,
> sleep were our losing, death our rhyme,

earth were the heavy fashion whence
we'd owe a curious innocence.
Then ours would be a stranger style,
in loveless bed a lonely while,
our bravery of afternoon
forgotten, and the desolate moon
drawn by the dead string's broken cry:
There never was an emptier sky!

Fitts dismissed the last line as "purest ham serene," and I dutifully recorded that put-down in my essay, figuring that if he disliked the line, it was probably defective. But I am older now, have published a fair number of books and, perhaps because of that, am confident enough to admit that I don't see anything wrong with it. It appears to me to be a perfectly plausible rhetorical representation of an emotional state, and if it doesn't tell us much about the sky, it does convey a good deal about the state of mind of the speaker in a hyperbole that is by no means inherently hammy. (Or, actually, it is the denial of the hyperbole, which is less extravagant but which still didn't pass muster with the poet.)

That talent Fitts had for witty deflation is something I remember vividly. There is a poem I wrote as an undergraduate that I liked well enough to include in my first collection, and I sent it off to Fitts because I was so pleased with it and with myself:

AS TRUE AS I STOOD

As true as I stood
in midwinter air, hearing the bells chime
so clear that they clappered into my chill blood
tart and sublime,

I have wished sincerely
to send on that numbing air a like rime
eve it, too, were to sound less and less clearly
with distance and time.

> If delight the bells give,
> always becoming, is always disappearing,
> and sound leaks through mind like rain through a great sieve
> and is soon out of hearing,
>
> a man—or some boy—
> then yanking the rope out of duty and all his breath
> had no time for time, ringing the bell in his joy,
> nor was bothered by death.

Well, it is windy and ambitious and probably too Dylan Thomas-y, and I didn't keep it in my *Selected Poems*, but what I most vividly and painfully remember about it is that Fitts sent it back to me with "tart and subliminal?" written in the margin at the end of the first stanza, ruining it so gleefully and so utterly that my retaining it for my first collection amounted to an act of willful defiance. He was right, of course. You never want to be unintentionally funny, and the tart/lime coincidence he had seized upon was all the more unfortunate in that it made it clearer that the line hadn't meant anything in particular in the first place. (Then, having turned against the piece myself, I couldn't help wondering what "chill blood" could mean and regretting that I'd settled for a rhyme on an adverb.)

You learn to write defensively, as you learn to drive defensively, always looking out for sudden wacky things those with whom you share the road are likely to do. But there is a limit beyond which caution becomes anxiety so that you can't even get into the car. In any case, with poetry, nobody gets hurt. The poem, if you make a mistake, may fail, but we have lots of poems.

The essay suggested that Small Susan was a real achievement, of "lasting" worth, and forty years on, I can report that it has, for me at least, lasted. It has stayed in my head; its jangle of hurt and anger that the weird diction embodied came to be more familiar to me than the twenty-two-year-old graduate student could have anticipated or would have wanted. There is, in *Equinox,* a poem of mine that is an homage to Fitts and Small Susan, "Rite for a Deceased Cat":

> We are all going to die—as all of us know,
> that knowledge being the penalty we pay
> for temporal lobes and the habit we've picked up
> of looking ahead in time, as animals don't.
>> ℣ Such unadorned statement of truth is not amusing.
>> ℟ A regrettable and, one hopes, infrequent lapse.

> They graze in grace those fields of here and now
> that we have lost. Hawks and vultures hover
> ever overhead in our clear air,
> or are they motes that float in nervous eyes?
>> ℣ One tried to avoid certain unpleasant subjects.
>> ℟ Milk or lemon in your nose, Mr. Morgan?

> Whether the fatty liver was cause or result
> of the anorexia, experts could not say.
> It seemed that the cat had retreated somewhere inward,
> her appetites sated at last, even for being.
>> ℣ I have, I fear, a subsequent engagement.
>> ℟ There is only one way to skin a cat.

> Her taste was for *nature morte.* The slightest movement
> affronted her eye, but a quick claw could fix it
> in a stillness which, in the end, she joined, herself.
> Light as a shadow, she now is a shadow's shadow.
>> ℣ A shadow in darkness. I shudder to think.
>> ℟ Precisely.

> Or, better, recall that watchful motionlessness
> with which she stalked a mole or squirrel or unwary
> bird. Imagine completion and perfection
> of that breathless poise: she does not need to pounce.
>> ℣ As my own pulse slows, the moment expands.
>> ℟ My eyelids narrow; my horizon widens.

Like an abandoned vessel, the body's bulk
wallows in heavier weather, loses way.
It takes a long time before she goes down.
We're moved but then lose interest and even patience.
    ℣ Never mind. It doesn't matter much.
    ℟ I couldn't have put it any better, myself.

Still, we miss her, admittedly less each day
as the expectation of her nimble lighting
on the foot of the bed diminishes. Heartlessness,
the hard lesson she teaches, we learn at last.
    ℣ Fastidiousness, and the grace to see what is.
    ℟ Pray for us at the hour of our death.

That book came out in 1989, and the poem must have been written in the mideighties, when I was fiftysomething. I still like it. I like the way it takes the awkward occasion of a cat's death, which is easily likely to turn mawkish, and toys with it. The versicles and responses are the same choragos and chorus that appeared in Fitts's poem, with the same odd outside-the-poem effect, and even, in one line, the same rhythm ("Precisely" for his "Profoundly"). And the resolution of the poem involves, I hope, a comparable diminution of a preceding dissonance.

Nabokov's line about writing for himself, his wife, and a few friends is probably darker than I realized. I thought he was being clubby and engagingly aloof as he put his audience at arm's length, albeit with a civil smile. What I realized later on was that "a few friends" would almost certainly include the dead, about whom we can say very little with any certainty, but who we assume must know a lot. Freed from the limitations of fashion, and even of time and mortality, they come to represent our ideas of enduring excellence. They are, after all, the ones whose memory has endured, and if they know anything it is about that. Excellence is what endures, isn't it?

That intimate and faithful audience, the writer's superego, his "few friends" are the ones he spends his life trying to please. In my small chorus, Fitts is one of the voices, often mocking, but at critical moments supportive and even affectionate. I have taken liberties with him or, reversing our old roles, have taught him a little of the forbearance and patience that might have been of benefit to him. The call to excellence is noble but it can be disabling, and I have somewhat mellowed that profane fury Fitzgerald remembered from the Choate chapel, just as I have revised and relaxed my father's rigid demands upon me that would have sent me to law school.

I was only sixteen when I first encountered Fitts in the basement classroom of Bullfinch Hall for English 4H, and his great gift to me was that he took me seriously. What was "deplorable" wasn't his poetry but mine, the novice work I would bring him for comment. The following year, when I got to Yale, the English department there let me do pretty much whatever I wanted because, as one of them told me, "You are one of Fitts's boys."

I still am.

Dr. Moore

ONE OF THE POETS DUDLEY Fitts brought up to Andover in 1951 and 1952 to read and talk to us about his poetry was Merrill Moore, who was probably the least well known of the Fugitives. An extraordinary man, he was a psychiatrist and a long-distance swimmer who wrote sonnets, lots of them. In a 1957 obituary, John Ciardi wrote that Moore was said to keep a pad on the dashboard of his car and that he had often written a sonnet while waiting for a traffic light to turn green. His big book, which came out in 1938 from Harcourt Brace, was called *M: One Thousand Autobiographical Sonnets*. Clearly, Fitts and Moore were old friends, for the acknowledgments page includes an expression of "deepest appreciation to John Crowe Ransom, Donald Davidson, Alfred Starr, Dudley Fitts, and Louis Untermeyer" for help in selecting and arranging the manuscript.

Having been alerted that Moore was coming, I went to the Oliver Wendell Holmes Library to get hold of a copy of one of his books, but Elizabeth Eades, the academy librarian, a formidable woman with a heavy southern accent, didn't approve of Dr. Moore's candor about sex and had withdrawn the book I wanted—almost certainly *Clinical Sonnets*—from general circulation. This meant that I had to get a note from Fitts directing her to let me borrow it.

I'd had problems with the library before. I'd been thrown out once for laughing out loud, which seemed to me very unfair. Laughter is not always under one's control, after all. And the reference room was almost empty at the time, so that my outburst wasn't so much an actual inconvenience to other scholars as it was a theoretical violation of the propriety and dignity of the library—which made it all the more important to the academy. What had occasioned my involuntary chortle was my reading of Cross's *Shorter History of England* in which I learned that "Gladstone's"—page break, followed on the verso by the rest of the sentence—"father was a greengrocer." And some wag, in straits as desperate as mine, had written in the margin, in pencil: "Very important! Will appear on exam!" After several hours of catching up on homework I'd deferred for far too long, that struck me with disproportionate force and I laughed. One of the reading room monitors, a white-haired assistant librarian, then came over to the table at which I was working, put her finger before her lips, scowled, and hissed *shhshhshh!* which also seemed funny, and I laughed aloud again. This was what got me sent to Dean Benedict's office for a mind-bendingly boring lecture on community spirit, a quality that prep school masters and gulag guards both value.

I mention this as a way of suggesting how I was particularly receptive to Dr. Moore's poetry. It was subversive. It, too, had been put under the ban by Elizabeth Eades. Assigned poetry may or may not be attractive to us, but poetry that has been forbidden has an undeniable glamour. It would be pleasant to suppose that Miss Eades was trying to promote our love of literature by keeping it from us—but I have no reason to think so. Andover was a fairly burly, anti-intellectual, even Philistine place, and few of the students were likely to request any of the books that she kept on the closed shelves.

Bizarrely enough, the only book I can remember my parents ever objecting to my reading had been *Crime and Punishment*, which my father thought was too morbid and depressing for a fifteen-year-old boy. (Nabokov detested that novel, too, but for other reasons: he thought it mawkish and sentimental.) I was dismayed, although not surprised, that Andover was monitoring what books the students were reading and was affirming the values of decency and propriety over those more challenging and uncomfortable ideals of freedom of inquiry and the right of artists to express themselves.

I have no idea which poems particularly bothered Miss Eades, or aroused in her worry about what they might to do us, and there are a number of possible candidates. My favorite among these is

You know what it means to be thoroughly satisfied?
Well, she was that, and it was the first time. It had
never happened to her before in her life. This experi-
ence she finally told me about. She was a stenographer,
born in Idaho. She moved to Indiana when she was 17
and had worked there for 10 years for one company

She was not good looking but she had a nice
Personality. Which she kept on ice.

On a Greyhound bus she met a young Diesel engineer
Who had been discharged that day from the U.S. Navy
After serving 39 months or so in the Pacific.

He was going to Chicago. He persuaded her
Somehow into a small second-rate hotel
Where they spent the seven days of her vacation
Mostly in bed, getting up to go out and eat.

She said it was the best vacation she ever had.
But it was more than a vacation; it was a conversion.
After 27 years she stopped living in corners,
Complained less about the high cost of living,
And let herself be invited to the party.

Incidentally she showed more interest in her work.

The first thing a reader is likely to notice about this poem is that the title is rather prolix. Moore's cheeky habit, which he freely confessed to us, was, if he had a sonnet that ran long, to put the extra lines in the title. This way, a seventeen-line poem, with the first three lines up there as a title, could still work out to fourteen. But this poem, this sonnet, still has a last line that violates the already violated form, an afterthought, a throwaway comment that is, like the couplets in a lot of Shakespeare's sonnets, anticlimactic but not altogether irrelevant. A psychiatrist friend of mine points out that the poem can also be understood as a counterpoint to psychoanalytic psychotherapy, with its tendency, back then, to regard action as somehow suspect. What Moore was maintaining as a nonanalytic therapist is that seven days in bed with a horny sailor can do more good than all that therapeutic talk. And, since the two great goals of the time were to be free in love and sex, he adds, with a smile and a nod to that agreed-upon agenda, that the "treatment" has also improved her functioning at work.

In a reprint Dudley Fitts gave me either before or just after Moore's visit to Andover of an essay about his friend that he'd published in *Sewanee Review* (in 1939), Fitts remarks about this gesture of the throwaway, which is not uncommon in Moore's work, saying:

> It must be confessed that this flatness is not always a conscious device. In many instances—perhaps in a majority of instances—the bathos-line is simply the result of careless composition; it is as though the author had tired of the poem before he had finished it, and had had recourse to any lame device to pad his stanza, achieve his rhyme. It is difficult to account for the ending of "While Atrafis was Walking" (524):
>
>> I must meet all of them tonight, remember
>> All I know—think nothing of it, chat
>> Of nothing, this and here and there and that.
>
> This is sheer let-down, the for-God's-sake-let's-get-it-finished feeling that is all too likely to intrude when Dr. Moore has made his point and found himself a line or two short. But the flat lines and phrases, when they work, are often more moving than many a showier poet's brilliancies.

It is difficult to disagree, but not impossible. By the midfifties, there were poets who, like Karl Shapiro, were beginning to be bored by the well-made poem, dissatisfied by the limitations of the small witty performance that came to be called "academic," and willing to take large risks for large effects. The Beats hadn't happened yet, but the constraints against which they were rebelling were already burdensome. And it was reassuring for me to see and hear this large, confident man with whom Fitts, constrained to the point of utter silence, was so clearly on friendly terms. Moore could make these rough, even crude gestures and, often get away with them, producing poetry that might be lacking in intricacy and deftness but that engaged the world somehow, taking notice of whatever chunks of experience floated by, and, in a hearty and sometimes impromptu prosiness, grappling with them. What Edgar Lee Masters had done in *Spoon River Anthology* or what Sherwood Anderson had done in *Winesburg, Ohio* Moore was doing in these sonnets. And the scale of the enterprise was such that if any particular sonnet was less than brilliant, it was nonetheless sustained by its setting among the other poems.

I remember Robert Penn Warren observing once in a class discussion at Yale that sentences of Theodore Dreiser were likely to be awkward but that they often combined into paragraphs that were less deplorable than one might have expected, while the larger unit of the chapter tended to be impressive—and a number of the novels were legitimately great. This may be interesting for readers, but liberating for writers, whose faith in themselves and the quality of their work is never altogether secure.

At any moment, you can look down at the sentence you've just written and ask yourself what you are doing and how you can have the temerity to go on. At such moments, Fitts's witty but withering remarks are not helpful, while Dreiser, and Moore, and Warren, too, are comforting presences.

Moore is all but forgotten now, except as a grace note in Robert Lowell's biography. Lowell was a manic depressive, and Moore was his psychiatrist and, for a time, his acting guardian. I am told that Moore was something of an outsider in Boston psychiatry, because he was looking for more efficient and economical ways of treating mental illness than analysis offered. It was Moore who took Lowell along with him on a trip back home to Nashville, Tennessee, to meet Allen Tate and John Crowe Ransom. Moore's mother lived nearby and part of his plan was that she could keep an eye on the young man. Moore also hired Robert Lowell's mother, Charlotte, as an office assistant, with duties that were mostly secretarial, but, as Ian Hamilton points out in his biography of Lowell, "after a time Moore allowed her to 'take on' a few of his milder 'cases.' Apparently, her brisk approach to mental illness could now and then jolt self-pitying society ladies into health."

The relationship between patient and psychiatrist is an intimate one, and "transference" is an important part of the dynamic. The patient cooperates in the treatment and makes progress toward mental health in part to please the therapist for whom he or she feels this important emotional connection. Lowell's relationship with Moore went beyond that of most psychiatrists with their patients. Indeed, it may have gone far beyond what is considered to be ethical. Paul Mariani says that Lowell resented the "intimacy" between his mother and Dr. Moore; the relationship may have been more than a purely professional one.

The literary consequence has always seemed clear to me—that Lowell's adoption of the rough sonnet form in his late work, particularly in *The Dolphin* and *Notebook*, had to be, at least in part, an homage to Moore. If John Berryman had begun to do this kind of thing in *Dream Songs*, Lowell could do his rough-hewn sonnets without feeling any obligation to Berryman (who was three years older), having Moore's example and authority from years before. The fourteen-line poem was also a convenience, a minimal formal requirement of having a fixed quantity of more or less iambic lines to be filled as gracefully as possible, an unconstraining constraint that was quietly reassuring.

What Lowell's later work amounted to is another question. I've never liked those poems of his, which seem to me graceless, self-indulgent, depressing, and depressed, the revelations of a personality that was unattractive, self-absorbed, and . . . well, crazy! (Of

course, they were all crazy—Berryman, Delmore Schwartz, Jean
Stafford, Randall Jarrell, and Lowell, preeminently, were all in and
out of mental hospitals.) Fitts said of Moore that he had a "passion-
ate humanity," and that he was "saying the lives of all of us." Lowell was saying only his own life, and much of that would have been
better left unsaid. Still, his later work goes back, I think, to Moore
and what he enabled, an alternative to an early correctness of Ransom and Tate that had come to be oppressive.

I take Moore's books down every so often, once or twice a
decade, and leaf through them. The poems, I think, hold up. He had
an eye for significant detail, a way not only of noticing these small
things but of delighting in them, and inviting us to share his delight.

> *His ambition: to have a cocktail named for him. He*
> *talked about it for years to all his friends but he died*
> *before his ambition was achieved*

The circumstances were not remarkable;
While drunk he drove his Packard off the road
One night about ten miles from Worcester, Mass.,

He struck a 150-year-old Yankee fence
Of boulders picked from the fields by pioneers
Where prior to that a glacier had put them down.

Some of them had been brought from Canada
By the glacier, some were Nova Scotia stone.

But anyhow they met and that was the end.
They met but did not mix, these ingredients
Of the cocktail he spent his life unsuccessfully
Trying to find and get bars to adopt.

I asked him once to define a cocktail for me;
He said: "a blend of liquors that develops a flavor of its own."

The tact, here, is in the decision to leave the obvious connections
to us to make. He offers us the *appellation d'origine* of the Nova Sco-

tia stone but resists the temptation to go as far as a use anywhere of
"on the rocks." My guess would be that Moore's influence on me has
been small but helpful. My own book-length sequence, *Dozens,* is
really a series of twelve-line stanzas that are deformed sonnets. If I
was lucky or pushed hard, I could get almost a sonnet's worth of
stuff into one of those stanzas. Or, if I wanted to be languid and relaxed, I could do one as a slow-motion octave. But as I think about it
now, I can see something of Moore's habit of understated closure in
some of the pieces, as, for instance, this:

83

The dignity of politics? The coronel
produces a very expensive fountain pen
from somewhere in his tunic, holds it up,
and asks what it can do. "A doctor, a judge,
or a general can kill with it, but a dentist
is a figure of fun because he seldom risks
his patients' lives. In times of peace and plenty,
politics also is trivial, but now . . ."
He unscrews the cap, stares at the broad gold nib,
and with a lethal flourish signs his bar chit.
"The crocodile, most of the time, is sleeping,
but when he wakes, there is sudden beautiful silence."

Winfield Townley Scott

IN A RECENT *TLS* COMMENTARY piece (February 22, 2002), Hugo Williams, a not at all bad British poet, writes about the reissue of an old travel book of his, *No Particular Place to Go,* and mentions the reviews it got when it originally appeared: "Apart from Auberon Waugh, who found it 'an empty, self-centered, rather unpleasant book,' and a young fogey called Anthony Bailey who hadn't heard of Lou Reed but chastised me for getting the middle name of the minor William Carlos Williams follower, Winfield Townly [*sic*] Scott, wrong, the reviews weren't bad."

My first reaction was mild pleasure in the validation of my fogey credentials, because I hadn't heard of Lou Reed either. Then I noticed that Williams still hadn't got Scott's middle name right. (Townley is not that difficult to find: a Google search produces the name, properly spelled, and the poet is in the Library of America anthology of twentieth-century American poetry.) And in any case, he wasn't a follower of William Carlos Williams but, if anyone, of Edward Arlington Robinson and Robert Frost. So poor old Scott has become the gold standard of obscurity, the kind of name *TLS* writers—and editors—feel comfortable about screwing up.

The word that stuck with me, though, was "minor," which hurt as much as anything else because it is probably true, and I have been thinking about what that means. Scott wasn't a bad poet, and certainly not an incompetent one. He was not perhaps adventurous either in technique or in sensibility, but he wrote a number of quite good poems. One of them I remember fairly clearly from his reading at Andover in early 1952, when Dudley Fitts had him come up and perform for us:

LANDSCAPE AS METAL AND FLOWERS

All over America railroads ride through roses.

I should explain this is thoroughly a matter of fact.
Wherever sandy earth is piled to make a road for train tracks
The banks on either side are covered with wild, sweet
Pink rambler roses: not because roses are pretty
But because ramblers grow in cheap soil and will hold
The banks firm against rain—therefore the railroad roses.

All over America the steel-supporting flowers,
Sometimes at village depots covering the shingled station,
Sometimes embracing watertanks, but mostly endless tendrils
Out of which locomotives and pullmans flash the morning—
And tunnels the other way into whose firm, sweet evening
The whistle fades, dragging freight cars, day coaches and the
    caboose.

What strikes me, still, is its modest plainspokenness, which is at the same time its virtue and its weakness. That move in the second line—"I should explain this is thoroughly a matter of fact."—is as antipoetic as one can get, but not inappropriate to the subject, which is the discovery of aesthetic pleasures in situations where that was not at all the intended result; to be more general about it, what Scott is talking about here is moments and occasions of grace.

It is only recently and at the prompting of the *TLS* reference that

I discovered that Scott Donaldson, the biographer of Fitzgerald, MacLeish, Cheever, and Hemingway, also did a biography of Winfield Townley Scott called *Poet in America* (published in 1972 by the University of Texas Press). It is an ominous title, I think, referring, perhaps, to Edgar Lee Masters's biography of Vachel Lindsay, a poet Masters very much admired and who had been, in John Hall Wheelock's words, "scorned and destroyed, allowed practically—he and his wife and children—to starve," so that, in the end, he committed suicide. In his preface, Donaldson explains his motive, which is what the title might lead us to expect: a story that "was in many ways characteristic of the not particularly happy condition of the artist in contemporary American society."

From Donaldson's book I learned that Winfield Scott's grandparents lived in a twin house in Haverhill, Massachusetts, in the other half of which the young Dudley Fitts lived with his mother and his sister. So Scott and Fitts knew each other from childhood and were probably the only living poets Haverhill had produced. In 1951, Scott came up to Haverhill for a Thanksgiving visit, at which time, according to Donaldson, he and Fitts renewed their boyhood acquaintance and Fitts invited Scott to Andover. During this visit I heard him read his poem "Mr. Whittier"—about John Greenleaf Whittier, who was also from Haverhill. I think he may have asked us whether we'd all read "Snowbound." Because he'd asked the question, I was emboldened to go up to him after the reading and mention to him that I had just written a parody of that poem (for a class in American literature, because it was less work than writing a critical paper). Scott was amused enough to ask me to send it to him and gave me his address.

That evening, I typed out a copy and put it into the mail, too delighted to wonder why he might have asked for it. I was quite surprised when he wrote back to say that he liked the poem and wanted to run it in the Sunday magazine section of the *Providence Journal,* where he had a column called "Bookman's Galley" and was the literary editor. Other than a few appearances on the children's page of the *White Plains Reporter Dispatch,* that was my first publication—although I'm pretty sure that the *Journal* didn't pay me anything for it. Still, I was delighted at having made my debut in such a way, with the approval of a poet who had appeared in John Ciardi's influential anthology, *Mid-Century American Poets*, along with such names, so much better known now, as Richard Wilbur, Muriel Rukeyser, Elizabeth Bishop, Karl Shapiro, Randall Jarrell, Delmore Schwartz, Theodore Roethke, and Robert Lowell.

It was a nice gesture, of course, and there's never any need to look into motives, but what strikes me now that I was unlikely to have realized back then was that I was probably only the incidental recipient of a kindness mostly intended for Fitts. What a nice thing to print one of his student's poems! And the readers of the paper would have been disarmed so that, if they liked the piece, they could applaud Scott for having found it, and if they didn't like it they could recognize his sporty generosity in giving a break to a high school kid. None of this means, however, that he didn't at least minimally like the poem, or that I am any the less grateful to him.

Donaldson's biography of Scott ought to be assigned reading in those creative-writing programs, a way of warning the would-be poets and writers what lies ahead. It wasn't a happy life. There was accomplishment and there was recognition, but never enough to satisfy Scott, whose life, at least in its external details, was in many ways enviable. He worked at the newspaper, which is a healthy thing to do, engaging the real world in a way that academic careers mostly don't. And his second wife, Eleanor Metcalf Scott, was the granddaughter of Jesse Metcalf, a textile mogul who bought a controlling interest in the *Providence Journal*. It was her money that allowed Scott to quit the paper. They had bought a two-hundred-year-old house just outside of Hampton, Rhode Island, a small town a few miles west of Providence that Scott thought looked like a re-creation of Grover's Corners in Thornton Wilder's *Our Town*. The house was on a dead-end road, and Winfield and Eleanor had spent a couple of summers there. In 1951, they hired a young architect who had studied with Gropius to modernize the place and make it more comfortable as a year-round house. Out in back, Eleanor had a ten-foot-by-ten-foot cedar shack built and equipped it with a woodstove, a desk, a dictionary, and a pencil sharpener so that her husband could work without being disturbed.

Heaven? Or one would think so. But as Donaldson reports, Scott was uneasy about it. He told an interviewer for *Yankee* magazine, "There is a great deal of sitting on the tail, waiting for things to get moving. An awful lot of looking out the window. But . . . I think there has to be all this apparent loafing and sitting around for eventual concentration." What bothered him was the bizarre idea that poetry is a job, that one should go and do it every day, and that if you don't write anything on a given day, then that day is a failure. "For the first time," Donaldson says, "Win was free to write, to work for himself and for whatever niche in posterity he might carve out, to strive full-time for the fulfillment of that ambition which had visited him in Haverhill High School more than a quarter century before."

What's odd is that I can understand how he felt, having been, myself, in a similar situation. When I left *Newsweek* in 1965 and moved to the Cape, it took me a while to adjust to the different rhythm of independent work. I had the misleading idea that a workday was eight or nine hours, but one should deduct from that span of time the meetings, the phone calls, and the administrative and clerical parts of almost any job that may be mildly tedious but from which there may be small satisfactions, and from which one can at least take a kind of reassurance. One is busy; one is doing something; one has put one more tedious chore behind him. Four hours of real work is a long day.

All of this seems too obvious to have to say or think, but what writers do requires an arrogance that Scott didn't have. He had doubts enough so that each day had to be justified—which is unreasonable. How many poems, after all, does one write in a lifetime? How many in a year? What's a reasonable quota, then, for a six-month period? Cutting it any finer than that is unfair and misleading.

At the Villa Serbelloni in Bellagio, poets who haven't learned these lessons go out into the woods into studies much like the one Eleanor built for Scott, and they sit there and listen to the clock tick as their four- or five-week residence slides by, and they feel inadequate and guilty. They lead lives that are difficult to imagine, that are difficult even for them to imagine as they sit there in their studios and wait for an idea to seize them. The beauty of the landscaping is almost an indictment, inviting them to perform, to respond, to memorialize. . . . Go ahead, do something! But poems don't want to be commanded that way. What's better is to ignore an idea the first time it presents itself, to wait and see if it comes back, if something else prompts it, as will almost certainly happen if the idea is connected in some way to what is important in the unconscious. What doesn't come back, what you can forget, is what you shouldn't have bothered with in the first place. Read, go for a walk, take a nap, go shopping, do something else. . . . (It's important to get out every day if only to keep depression at bay.)

Harry Cohn, of Columbia Pictures, is said to have gone sometimes into the writers' building and to have bellowed, "What's the matter? I want to hear them typewriters going!" That's an old bit of Hollywood lore that is supposed to demonstrate what boors the studio heads were. But writers can be just as boorish with themselves. For those of us who write novels, or translate, or do nonfiction, there can be a kind of Stakhanovite satisfaction in reliably grinding out another couple of pages, but Scott didn't do any of that. He was a poet, writing poetry, in this dreamworld cabin out in the woods behind this elegantly refurbished seventeenth-century house. And that, it turns out, is a precarious and vertiginous job to try to do full-time. Rejections from magazines and book publishers upset him disproportionately. It is never easy to be turned down, but unless one is prepared to follow Emily Dickinson's perfectly sensible regimen and write poems that one then puts into a drawer, there is always the risk of rejection, and there is always someone else who seems to be doing better, getting more and better reviews, selling more, and getting prizes and awards. Scott wrote to Horace Gregory a slightly paranoid note about how some of his fellow poets were "sucking up to editors and anthologists," and complaining about "the homosexual links" that seemed to be governing decisions down in New York, and he asked, quite reasonably, "but don't all these people see that all this activity is nothing? That the only thing that lasts, the only thing that counts, is the work itself, well done?" If only he had believed that, or had believed it more deeply.

He did a little book reviewing for the *New York Herald Tribune*—which I did, too, when I left *Newsweek*—and he had an offer from *Time* to be a part-time reviewer. This would have meant coming into

New York every Friday for a book conference, and he was tempted, and figured that it was like having a "permanent double Guggenheim," but he turned it down because he didn't want to "skimp" on the poetry. This was probably a mistake.

He groused, and he stewed, and he drank a lot. In Russell A. Fraser's *A Mingled Yarn: The Life of R. P. Blackmur*, Delmore Schwartz is reported to have observed that he never in all his life saw anyone as drunk as Winfield Townley Scott—which is like an NBA player's remark that someone struck him as impressively tall. Scott also worried a lot about living on his wife's money and defined himself as a kept man. As he observed in a remark that was not altogether a joke, his son Joel was paying more in taxes than he was.

Part of this feeling of insecurity was, no doubt, social. One of the paradoxical gifts of feminism is that the redefinition of gender roles has been helpful to men, too. I have sometimes startled my students by telling them that I have the life every Vassar girl in the fifties dreamed of—I married a doctor and I have my hobby. I also have the Jewish tradition to call on, in which the women looked after the business while the men went off to the study house to discuss arcane Talmudic matters. Neither of these cushions was available to Scott, however, and he felt bad. He thought he was obligated to produce and to succeed, and then, when he wasn't writing a lot or was having trouble placing what he'd written, he felt worse. But then, when good things happened, they didn't help him much. He and Eleanor moved to Santa Fe, where the constraints of New England Puritanism were less oppressive and traditional gender roles could be ignored. Donaldson cites a letter of Scott's that observed, "The boy-and-boy, woman-and-woman arrangements are notable. They live together and run shops together; nothing much is made of it; some—both sorts—we are friends with are pleasant, seemingly unpredatory—settled." And he was not despised or ignored. In 1966, for instance, he got word that *Poetry* had given him the Harriet Monroe Memorial Award for the year, gave several successful readings, and then learned from David Wagoner that he would share in the Helen Bullis Memorial Prize of *Poetry Northwest*. It was also the year when his *New and Selected Poems* was published by Doubleday, and Sam Vaughan, writing as "L. L. Day, Editor at Large," said in the ad in the *New York Times Book Review* that Scott was "overdue for the Pulitzer Prize in poetry and/or the National Book Award." And he had a very enthusiastic review by Hayden Carruth that compared his talent to that of Robert Frost.

He was nonetheless miserable, depressed enough to consult a psychiatrist, drinking too much, worried about his declining sexual powers, but most centrally suffering what can only be described as a crisis of faith, for that belief in "the only thing that counts . . . the work, itself, well done" wasn't strong enough to keep his doubts about himself at bay.

One could argue that with contemporary pharmacology, with some Wellbutrin maybe, and some Viagra, Scott's life might have been better, or at least a little less intolerable. Still, the po' biz is a tough racket, and editors seldom take into account the fragility of their betters. Friends of mine report that Peter Davison had solicited poetry from Winfield Scott, who had promptly replied with a selection of things—all of which were returned, not even with a note but just a printed *Atlantic Monthly* rejection slip.

Whether that was the last straw or not, it certainly couldn't have helped. He complained about it bitterly. And in the early morning hours of April 28, 1968, just two days shy of his fifty-eighth birthday, he went out to the guest house with a bottle of liquor and a smaller bottle of five-hundred-milligram capsules of Placidyl (a now discontinued short-term hypnotic, or, in plain language, sleeping pills). While he didn't take all the pills in the bottle, he took enough of them so that, with what he'd had to drink, intentionally or not, he killed himself.

The work that remains deserves better than the contempt of the *TLS*. It is poetry I want to like, which is reasonable enough. We often come to literature with a certain bias, sometimes favorable, more often antagonistic. A writer whose success we at first applauded seems suddenly to be boring, or not to have lived up to the hype with which we have grown impatient, and we don't want to blame ourselves for having been taken in, so we blame him or her. There are other, smaller hostilities we may bring as individuals to a writer's work. I can think of a number of novelists and poets who have be-haved badly—to me or to friends of mine—and I am willing to admit to my delight in their bad reviews.

What Scott gets from me, then, is attention, so that I open his books now and then. But I'm not blind to his faults, the main one of which is that he probably wrote too much. Or having written too much, he kept too much of it. The wastebasket can be a writer's best friend. But if he was out there in that studio, that dreamworld atelier his wife had put up for him, and if he felt that his enviable freedom had to be justified every day, it would have been hard for him to throw things away.

He had ambition, which is a peculiar quality in a poet. He was, as Hugo Williams accurately observed, a "minor" poet, which is what most of us are. Major poets are cultural accidents, the results of ran-dom coincidences of individual talent and a culture's need for certain things to be expressed at a certain time and in a certain way. A poet's ambition ought to be both more rigorous and more modest than Scott could afford to be. He should be satisfied by writing as well as he can. Excellence is a better goal than "majority" anyway, if only because we have a slightly less murky idea of what excellence is.

Scott has poems that qualify as excellent, passing the most scrupu-lous muster. There are many of them that I can like without qualifi-cation or embarrassment, and quite a few I can reread with admiration and gratitude. Scott was, himself, able to tell, for the title poems of each of his collections are all particularly accomplished. One I'm fond of, a novel idea executed with great panache, is "To Marry Strangers," which takes as its donnée a husband coming across a childhood photograph of his wife:

> Since after all we were born to marry strangers—
> O child, child, child that I never knew!—
> Is this photograph of a child I have begotten
> And forgotten? Or is it you?
>
>   Or is it true
> Love alive is no more retroactive
> Than sure of any future? But though it may

Imagine you both beautiful and gray
Cannot, the other way, return and find you?
Where would it find you? This child, this
Beloved stranger? Unconceived daughter? Who?
This is wild—this riddles reason,
This leap of leaves storming off the ground—
Their turning from gold to green is wild
Yet I love this child—would go to her, hold her—
Wherever she could be found.

                                But no, but no:
The leaves are never still, they fall all seasons.
And none, none, none resumes the bough.
That alone which is lost will find what is lost,
And you are here, and I: and in this noon
Not even small ghosts run. Across the sun
No voice bends back the wind. But always the wind
Lifts your hair and all the sun is shaken,
And yet may lift it colorless in the moon,
And I—in so much blest—alone remember
The light that moves upon your strange face now.

He deserves better, surely, than to be a butt of British jokes. His bad
luck holds, though, for he wrote in a time when poets' reputations
had a marginal viability. Back in the fifties, there was a normal pro-
gression by which at least some of the poetry that undergraduates
and graduate students liked would work its way into the curriculum
as those young men and women got jobs as instructors and then
worked their way up the academic ladder. English majors might not
be the smartest youngsters on the campus, but they liked literature
and were enthusiastic about some of the things they read. That
changed in the sixties. By then, a college education was no longer a
privilege but had become an obligation, a requirement for admission
into the middle class. And then, during the Vietnam War, enrollment
in some institution of higher education was an alternative to getting
shot at. Not unreasonably, there were youngsters who found them-

selves on campuses without any enthusiasm, and, indeed, often with resentment. They were angry at their parents and at the institutions, and that anger has now become an official part of the curriculum. The "canon" has suffered. There is no generally agreed-upon body of texts or group of writers whom the professors of literature assign to students. The photocopying machine has further eroded the illusion of a collective set of writings, for each instructor invents his or her own textbook and teaches whatever he or she likes most (or hates least).

Who reads Nemerov anymore, or Delmore Schwartz? And what kind of chance does Scott have in so unhealthy an environment?

I very much doubt that an essay like this one can reverse the tide for him. Still, I owe his memory this small favor. Or, say, that I owe Fitts, and that Scott is the incidental beneficiary. As I was, once.

I have the same kinds of hedges that he had. If you like what you've read here of his work, then you give me a little credit for bringing it to your attention. And if not, then you think I'm a sporty guy, giving him a break this way—or very smart, writing about so arcane and obscure a fellow as he has become.

"An Anatomy of the World: The First Anniversary" by John Donne

A SOPHOMORE AT YALE, I first read this poem in Bill Madsen's seminar in seventeenth-century literature in the fall of 1953. He was a fine teacher, careful, responsible, much more scholarly than I was or am, but with a sense of humor and also, as I remember, a sense of proportion, which is not something one always finds among academics. He understood what some scholars can't or won't—that these poems we read are not merely historical documents or "texts," pretexts for analysis and performance, but works of art with an importance that comes from their effectiveness and accomplishment in a domain quite different from that of the classroom. I cannot recall his ever having formulated his thoughts in just this way, but he brought to our conversations about the poems before us a modesty and an enthusiasm that ought to be fundamental to literary criticism.

I can no longer recall exactly what he had to say about "An Anatomy of the World," but I would have been able to remember his remarks only if they had been tendentious or grating, some misprision of the poem. I was not the kind of student who took orderly notes, or, except in rare instances, any at all. Indeed, I prided myself in not lugging a notebook about but instead relying almost entirely on a green plastic Mickey Mouse bookmark that I had tucked into my textbooks and that had a dull surface on the back on which one could write in pencil, so that I could jot down assignments and then, when they were done, erase them.

My inability to regenerate any of Bill Madsen's comments seems to me not only understandable but in an odd way laudable and entirely proper. After all, it was never his purpose in discussing this or any other poem to call attention to himself, to try to assert himself or to stake his claim upon it, seizing it from its author. Harold Bloom had not yet made his impertinent remark about how "a strong misreading is the equivalent of a new poem," and New Haven in the early fifties was a much more civil place than it would become in a decade or so. Madsen never said so, but my impression was that transparency was one of his aims as he directed our attention not to himself but to John Donne and, most important, to the poem on the page before us, its nuances and techniques, its matter and manner.

I read the poem again, only a few years later, at Columbia, in a graduate class with Marjorie Hope Nicolson, who was the department chairwoman and an eminent academic. I was at Columbia more or less by accident. I'd married in August 1956 and had gone off to spend a year in Florence, where I'd persuaded my parents and in-laws that I could accomplish as much there in preparing myself to be a writer as I could by spending the same time in Iowa, where Paul Engle had invited me to come out to study creative writing. Iowa or . . . Florence? The cornfields or the Piazza della Signoria?

My wife and I had got as far as Paris when the news reached us that her mother had had a stroke and died. We came back for the funeral and decided that Florence didn't make sense any longer. We'd move in with my father-in-law in Plainfield, New Jersey. And I would go to graduate school, for a year anyway, earn a master's degree, and decide then what I wanted to do. It was the bus schedules that made Columbia look more attractive and convenient than Princeton. I went to Columbia to ask the admissions people what the chances were of my studying there—the term would start in a week or so. They asked whether I had an undergraduate degree. When I assured them that I had a Yale BA, magna cum laude, and explained that we'd just come back from Europe because of a death in the family, they allowed as how, if I went up to New Haven, got a transcript, found a couple of people willing to write me letters of recommendation, and got all this back to them by five o'clock that day, they'd let me know the next Monday.

I took a cab to 125th Street, caught the next New York, New Haven, and Hartford train back to Yale, and took another cab to the registrar's office, where I was told that it would take three days for them to generate a transcript. I told them what the people had told me at Columbia and explained that I needed the document in three hours. And someone there decided that I was not insane and that, considering what the exigencies were, they could copy out my transcript by hand. I thanked them and left the office to wander the streets looking for two or three familiar faces who could supply those letters of recommendation that Columbia required, writing them out on tables at coffee shops or, in one instance, on my back.

Jacques Barzun, whom I never met but who was teaching at Columbia at the time, observes in *The Culture We Deserve* that "we give degrees that supposedly certify excellence and then require stacks of letters of recommendation in order to distinguish real merit from the rest." When I read these words, it crossed my mind that what Professor Barzun hadn't bothered to say was that a diploma is, itself, actually a letter of recommendation addressed to "All Those to Whom These Presents May Come" and signed by the president and the secretary of the university, but that these have been so devalued that, without particular endorsements from known individuals recertifying what the diploma says, they are more or less worthless except as certificates of nonexclusion.

Columbia's master's degree program was, I suspect, a money-making operation and, secondarily, a recruitment tool for those whom the departments may later admit as doctoral candidates. It was a more or less relaxed operation in which the students didn't actually have to show up very often. There were no course grades and no one kept track of attendance. One paid one's money (or one's parents' money), and this qualified him or her to sit for the two-day comprehensive exam and turn in a master's essay. I generally went up to

New York once a week to attend Richard W. B. Lewis's proseminar. The master's essay I wrote for him was about the original poetry of Dudley Fitts, who had been a teacher of mine at Phillips Academy and who had written one slender book of verse—*Poems, 1929–1936*. I was interested in his work mostly because of its minimal demands: there were fifty pages or so of text and no secondary material of any kind, and I could consult Fitts if I had to about the meaning of some of these odd and even wifty poems of his. There was a deeper interest, though, in that I was frightened by the example of a man of enormous cultivation and impressive talent who could start out with a book like this, publishing with New Directions this one slender volume, and then . . . Give up? Fail? Turn to the classics and just not feel like writing original poetry anymore?

There were some weeks when I'd venture in just to check on those classes for which I was registered and that I was theoretically attending. James Clifford's class in eighteenth-century literature was first rate and worth the hour-long trip on the bus. William York Tindall's class in modern lit was quirky and sometimes annoying but lively enough for me to drop in on now and then. I have the impression that I might have been in Mark Van Doren's class, but I don't remember going to it or even what the class was about. I may not even have had a class with him, and it may be merely a trick of memory— I knew him, slightly, later on and might have persuaded myself that I'd had a ghostly appearance in a class he taught. The arithmetic works out, though. Nicolson, Clifford, Tindall, Lewis, and Van Doren add up to five, which sounds like a normal academic schedule.

Marjorie Nicolson was a formidable enough woman to have succeeded in Columbia's male clubbiness. It didn't strike me at the time as at all unusual, but she was probably the only woman in Columbia's English department. (And my guess is that in the departments at Yale, Harvard, Princeton, and Brown back then there wouldn't have been any women at all.) If Trilling was Columbia's Jew, she was their female. And she did it through earnest and reliable scholarship in intellectual history. So she went at the Donne poem—I came in, as I say, from time to time, and happened to catch this lecture—worrying it as if she were a terrier playing with an old slipper and focusing almost entirely on the two lines about how "New philosophy calls all in doubt, / The element of fire is quite put out . . ." And then, studiously, professorially, she explicated what Donne was referring to, attending more to the intellectual and scientific history than to the poetry and informing us what great changes were happening and what the discontinuities were in worldview from what had prevailed the generation before.

To be fair to her, it was a course for graduate students, and I suppose that she might have assumed we had all read the poem and responded to it in the primary way. Still, does one ever read a poem, particularly a great poem, without any aesthetic response? And I can't recall any coloration of excitement or admiration or awe in her comments. She may, of course, have been suppressing as gushy and amateurish those kinds of displays that were more feminine than she thought she could afford. I remember only being impressed and distressed at the same time, by the intellectual dazzle that had little to do with the business the poem is transacting with readers.

During the forty-four years or so since then, I have opened my Donne from time to time, have read here and there, for the tune of it, to remind myself of the authority of his bravura openings ("For God's sake hold your tongue, and let me love," or "Busy old fool, unruly sun,"), but I had not gone back to examine this poem until I found myself teaching a course at Bennington College in English religious poetry of the seventeenth century. I'd volunteered to do this even though I am not a specialist (Bennington doesn't believe in specialists), because I thought that such a course ought to be offered to the students, would be good for them, and would, in fact, be good for me. An occasion to go back and look hard at the work of such poets as Donne, Herbert, Crashaw, Vaughan, Marvell, and Milton, as well as John Owen, Edward Taylor, and the Countess of Pembroke was attractive indeed. And one of the best ways of taking such a course is up at the front of the room, in the teacher's chair.

I was startled to discover how much the poem had changed, or, more accurately, how much my understanding of it had changed. It had been a knotty, dense text with a general downwardness (which, as I recalled, was answered by the general upwardness of the companion poem, "Of the Progress of the Soul: The Second Anniversary"), but now it was much clearer, much more a comprehensible expression of the torment of grief or even a "reactive depression," the kind one experiences in reaction to some external event, most often a death.

In the Norton Critical Edition, which is a selection of the poems and essays about poems in wide use in college classes, Frank Manley's essay about the Anniversaries attributes to Marjorie Nicolson the observation that these are perhaps two sections of what is, in effect, the same poem, and I was pleased to realize that perhaps I had remembered something of her lectures, after all. Manley cites her comments that she had published in 1950—just a few years before I took her class—about how "The Anniversaries are . . . as artfully though not so obviously articulated as 'L'Allegro' and 'Il Penseroso.' The first is a lament over the body—the body of man and the body of the world—a meditation upon death and mortality. The second is a vision of the release of the soul from its prison. The whole, with antitheses of doubt and faith, despair and hope, death and the triumph of immortality, is a great symphony in which the harmony is more profound because of cacophony."

Manley also refers to Louis Martz's suggestion, in *The Poetry of Meditation*, that both poems grow out of a "deliberately articulated structure" which is not elegiac but meditative, based on the principles of meditation established by Ignatius Loyola. Martz, Manley reports, "regarded the poems as only partially successful. In The Second Anniversary . . . the meditative structure is organic; in The First, it is mechanical. One poem therefore is a success, the other a qualified failure."

I never took a course with Louis Martz, but I knew him at Yale when I was an undergraduate, and we are still friendly. I actually reviewed *The Poetry of Meditation* in the *Yale Daily News* when it was first published (which seems like a cheeky thing for me to have done as a nineteen-year-old junior, but, as I recall, I was enthusiastic about the book and recognized that it was a startlingly different and accurate way of reading many of these poems). There are a great many tripartite meditative poems of this period where Martz's application of the machinery of meditation in the practice of Loyola and of Saint Francis de Sales is not only helpful but revelatory, demonstrating a whole way of thinking that is now remote from our ordinary repertoire and that helps us understand the poems more clearly. (The three sections of the paradigmatic "meditative" poem would be a "composition of place," an "exercise of understanding," and then an "exercise of judgment and will.")

Martz's view, however, is that "The First Anniversary" doesn't fit this meditative pattern comfortably, has awkward and abrupt transitions, and only tangentially connects the general despair of the speaker's view of the world to the death of Elizabeth Drury, whose demise is the ostensible occasion of the poem. There is, of course, another possibility, which is that the poem doesn't fit the formula but nevertheless succeeds in other ways and with other aims, that its quirky development is mimetic of a jangled psychological state, and that the extravagant hyperbole of the poem is a way of representing the extremity of feeling of someone in the grip of grief or depression. And with this reading, "The Second Anniversary" would be a depiction of the healed soul of a year later, which is, clinically, about right, if the sufferer is not afflicted by what Freud calls "complicated grief."

My reading of the poem was neither helped nor marred by any thesis or theory. One of the advantages of that Mickey Mouse bookmark was that it was a way of preserving the innocence with which I used to read and which any writer wants his readers to bring to bear on his poems. I was a smart enough kid to have learned how to perform in English classes, but I was also aware that these performances could often get in the way of my relationship to poems. I was, even then, trying to maintain my amateur standing. I did have—and still have—certain technical requirements that are mostly negative: that the poetry ought not be clumsy or inept; that the workmanship not obtrude or distract; that there be a display of trustworthy syntactical and metrical competence. But mostly, my aim is, and I think even then was, to be open and simple, acknowledging my aesthetic and emotional reactions as well as whatever intellectual connections the poem may enable or demand.

Martz is quite clear in his judgment that after line 284, "the best of the poem is over," which seems to me wrongheaded, particularly with such passages as follow on the subject of proportion. The speaker is not stupid and is quite aware of the fact that his sense of himself and the world can no longer be trusted.

The world's proportion disfigured is,
That those two legs whereon it doth rely,
Reward and punishment are bent awry.
And, oh, it can no more be questioned,
That beauty's best, proportion, is dead,
Since even grief itself, which now alone
Is left us, is without proportion.
She by whose lines proportion should be
Examined, measure of all symmetry,
Whom had that ancient seen, who thought souls made
Of harmony, he would at next have said
That harmony was she, and thence infer
That souls were but resultances from her,
And did from her into our bodies go
As to our eyes, the forms from objects flow:
She, who if those great Doctors truly said
That the Ark to man's proportions was made,
Had been a type for that, as that might be
A type of her in this, that contrary
Both elements, and passions, lived at peace
In her, who caused all civil war to cease.
She after whom, what form soe'er we see,
Is discord, and rude incongruity;
She, she is dead, she's dead; when thou know'st this
Thou know'st how ugly and monster this world is . . .

This is by no means failed poetry, even if it doesn't quite fit Martz's precise schema. The anger we have at the death of someone we've loved, whose loss contradicts all orderly sense of reward and punishment and all reason in the world—why is she dead and why are all these people on the streets still alive?—is acute and agonizing, and even though we understand that our anger isn't rational, that doesn't make it go away. And if one is a writer, one's questioning of one's reason and judgment is all the more disturbing, because the work is what we have to hold on to, and even that is now suspect: how can we trust what we write if our thoughts and feelings are out of control and at odds with what we have thought and felt in the past?

But I am getting ahead of myself. The poem starts with what the side gloss tells us is "The entry into the work," presenting us with the death that is its cataclysmic occasion:

> When that rich soul which to her heaven is gone,
> Whom all they celebrate, who know they have one,
> (For who is sure he hath a soul, unless
> It see, and judge, and follow worthiness,
> And by deeds praise it? He who doth not this,
> May lodge an inmate soul, but 'tis not his.)
> When that Queen ended here her progress time,
> And, as t'her standing house, to heaven did climb,
> Where, loath to make the saints attend her long,
> She's now a part both of the choir, and song,
> This world, in that great earthquake languished;
> For in a common bath of tears it bled,
> Which drew the strongest vital spirits out:
> But succoured then with a perplexed doubt,
> Whether the world did lose, or gain in this,
> (Because since now no other way there is
> But goodness, to see her, whom all would see,
> All must endeavor to be good as she,)
> This great consumption to a fever turned,
> And so the world had fits; it joyed, it mourned.

The issue Frank Manley finds interesting to explore is the meaning of Elizabeth Drury's death. We know that Elizabeth was the only surviving daughter of Sir Robert Drury of Hawstead, Suffolk, who died in December 1610 at the age of fourteen, and that Donne never met her—although his sister Anne had known the Drurys for some years and probably encouraged Donne to write about Elizabeth in order to attract Sir Robert's patronage.

Manley alludes to Ben Jonson's report of what Donne said to him, "that he described the Idea of a Woman and not as she was," but, as Manley says, "the problem then becomes, what is she a symbol of?" And to solve this riddle, he brings into play a great many pieces of literary and intellectual heavy equipment from "the possibilitatem boni Augustine thought was lost in the fall" back to Plato's notion of the completion of the androgynous soul and on through to C. G. Jung's concept of anima. All of that seems to me mildly interesting but somehow beside the point. The falling apart of the world or the clear understanding of the sickness of the world that Donne describes is not at all recherché or in any way foreign to those who have suffered the grief of the death of a loved one. The loss one feels is, almost by definition, of something—someone— valuable, precious, virtuous, and irreplaceable. Elizabeth Drury's death was in that way like almost any death, a perfectly plausible occasion for an expression of the kind of despair that can seize any of us when the firm ground of ordinary experience opens beneath our feet and we stare down, perhaps for the first time, into the abyss before us. The world's persistence in indifference and apparent health is an affront.

Donne is simply describing the way many bereaved people have felt when he continues:

> And, as men think, that agues physic are,
> And th'ague being spent, give over care,
> So thou, sick world, mistak'st thyself to be
> Well, when alas, thou 'rt in a lethargy.
> Her death did wound and tame thee then, and then
> Thou mightst have better spared the sun, or man;
> That wound was deep, but 'tis more misery,
> That thou has lost thy sense and memory.
> 'Twas heavy then to hear thy voice of moan,
> But this is worse, that thou are speechless grown.
> Thou has forgot thy name, thou hadst; thou wast
> Nothing but she, and her thou has o'erpast.

That sense of outrage that the world persists apparently unchanged is perhaps a hyperbole but it is a widespread perception. My dear friend Fred Chappell wrote a poem and dedicated it to me about my reaction to my mother's murder (which we had never discussed) and, now that I think of it, his short poem sketches quickly and quietly the general motion of Donne's First and Second Anniversaries:

MESSAGE

for David Slavitt

True:

   the first messenger angel may arrive
purely clothed in terror, the form he takes
a swordblade of insuperable energies,
making the air he entered a spice of ozone.

And then the mad inventories. Each trait
of nature, each animal and flower and pretty bird,
is guilty of persistence. The tear of sorrow,
huge as an alien star, invades
our sun's little system.

       Irrelevant
such enormity: because the man is alone
and naked. Even the tenuous radiations
of the marauding star crush him like falling timbers.
The worst is, he must choose among sorrows
the one that destroys him most.

But see how all changes in that hour.

He ascends a finer dimension of event, feels with senses
newly evolved the long horizons unknown till now.
He is transformed head to foot, taproot to polestar.
He breathes a new universe, the blinding whirlpool
galaxies drive round him and begin to converse.

Those last six lines, I am afraid, are more hortatory or optative than declarative, but the sense is clear, and it can happen that one's horizons do expand. At the very least, I am better equipped to understand Donne's poem than I was before.

Donne goes on to set up the overarching conceit of the poem, which is that the world itself is dead and that he is anatomizing it, performing what we now call an autopsy, for the readers' instruction:

I (since no man can make thee live) will try,
What we may gain by thy anatomy.

Her death hath taught us dearly, that thou art
Corrupt and mortal in thy purest part.
Let no man say, the world itself being dead,
'Tis labor lost to have discovered
The world's infirmities, since there is none
Alive to study this dissection;
For there's a kind of world remaining still,
Though she which did inanimate and fill
The world, be gone, yet in this last long night,
Her ghost doth walk; that is, a glimmering light,
A faint weak love of virtue and of good
Reflects from her, on them which understood
Her worth; and though she have shut in all day
The twilight of her memory doth stay;
Which, from the carcase of the old world, free
Creates a new world; and new creatures be
Produced: the matter and the stuff of this,
Her virtue, and the form our practice is.

Andrew Solomon observes in *The Noontime Demon* that in a depression one has the sense that a veil has been torn from one's eyes and that the bleakness one encounters is the truth, and my hunch is that he is responding to the same kind of experience as that which Donne describes.

This new world may be safer, being told
The dangers and diseases of the old:
For with due temper men do then forgo,
Or covet things, when they their true worth know.
There is no health; physicians say that we
At best, enjoy but a neutrality.
And can there be worse sickness, than to know
That we are never well, nor can be so?
We are born ruinous: poor mothers cry
That children come not right nor orderly,
Except they headlong come, and fall upon
An ominous precipitation.

One important difference between ordinary depression and one associated with and occasioned by a death is that those who have been bereaved have a disincentive about recovery: they want to hold on to their grief as a last and therefore all the more precious remnant of the person for whom they mourn. This condition presents itself, therefore, not merely as a psychological but also an intellectual and even a theological disease.

Donne's intellectual and theological display of the next sixty or seventy lines is what academics love: they can explicate away, imparting pieces of information that the poem may seem to require. The notes in any reasonable edition are, of course, quite adequate to explain the references and present the ideas with which Donne is playing here, but what they don't explain is that he is playing, that this is a kind of legerdemain, an impressive dazzle that we are not to take too seriously. Indeed, the unseriousness of it is what is, in large measure, so impressive—as in Donne's argument in "The Flea," which is intricate and elaborate but altogether absurd (the flea has bitten you, has bitten me, has mingled our bloods in its body, so that we are therefore married—and might as well now have sexual relations!).

Here, the intellectual display is not absurd on its face, but that doesn't mean we are obliged to trust it absolutely. The speaker is distracted, distraught, and in his torment and disgust he is giving us a cosmological description the purpose of which is characterization of the speaker more than accuracy about the external world. The idea is that Eve's sin brought death into the world and that we are now fallen and, during the course of history, have diminished even further ("who lives to age, / Fit to be made Methusalem his page?"). Mankind, the speaker goes on to say, has been saved by Christ's coming, but that, though necessary, may not have been sufficient.

> This man, whom God did woo, and loth t' attend
> Till man came up, did down to man descend,
> This man, so great, that all that is, is his,
> Oh what a trifle, and poor thing he is!
> If man were anything, he's nothing now:
> Help, or at least some time to waste, allow
> T' his other wants, yet when he did depart

With her whom we lament, he lost his heart.
She, of whom th' ancients seemed to prophesy,
When they called virtues by the name of *she*,
She in whom virtue was so much refined,
That for allay unto so pure a mind
She took the weaker sex, that she could drive
The poisonous tincture, and the stain of Eve,
Out of her thoughts, and deeds; and purify
All, by a true religious alchemy;
She, she is dead; she's dead; when thou know'st this,
Thou know'st how poor a trifling thing man is.

This is, as I think Nicolson held, a critical moment in which Elizabeth Drury becomes another Mary, whom we would expect to find as the usual counter to Eve in this situation, as the redemption is the counter to the fall. Nicolson thought it was a rhetorical difficulty requiring the formulation of a theory of the "double She," the dead girl and the ghostly presence that is either the classical virtues or perhaps an Anglican version of Mariolatry, very slightly disguised because it was such an extravagant stretch. Donne's leap, though, seems quite reasonable to me, a plausible indication of the pain of the speaker and his distraction.

The poem could quite reasonably have ended here, at the 184th line, but Donne goes on and lets these two lines become a refrain that holds together a long jeremiad about the general mess of things, the woe that the bereft speaker finds in all things that conforms to and confirms the woe in his own heart. Just after the disasters of September 11, I spoke with my sister and we were talking about the change in the public mood and discourse, the hurt and anger and grief that the media were trying without much success to find some way to express. I told her that the country now feels the way we felt when our mother was killed. There was a pause while she thought about that. And then a simple, terrible, "Yes."

That refrain line, with its wrenched and stammering syntax ("She" is repeated three times), comes back with the dull thud of a funereal drum, not with any predictable periodicity, but often enough so that one learns to expect it, or fear it. It is not mere punctuation, but what

the grief counselors call a STUG—a Sudden Temporary Upsurge of
Grief that can, at any moment, sneak up to clutch one and produce a
fresh sensation of pain and a gush of tears. Its first reappearance is
roughly fifty lines on:

> She that was best, and first original
> Of all fair copies; and the general
> Steward to Fate; she whose rich eyes, and breast,
> Gilt the West Indies, and perfumed the East;
> Whose having breathed in this world, did bestow
> Spice on those Isles, and bade them still smell so,
> And that rich Indy which doth gold inter,
> Is but as single money, coined from her:
> She to whom this world must itself refer
> As suburbs, or the microcosm of her,
> She, she is dead; she's dead: when thou know'st this,
> Thou know'st how lame a cripple this world is.

Then there are a hundred lines or so before we see the line again,
and the effect is an odd one. At the first appearance, it is a striking
line. The second time, it is a reprise and plays differently because it
is familiar and we recognize it, realizing now that it is not merely a
line of verse but a structural element. From then on, we expect it, but
that expectation is not fulfilled for rather a long time, during which
we are expecting it, waiting for it, uneasy even, because it is in our
minds while we are reading, always there in a ghostly way, informing whatever else we are reading—just as the memory of the deceased is always there, and the feeling of loss.

Very few undergraduates have the kind of experience to bring to
their reading that would let them know how accurate an enactment
the poem is of the ache of bereavement and the soul-sickness that can
attend upon a loss. Elizabeth Drury, let us remember, was fourteen
when she died, and even if the Elizabethans and Jacobeans were better inured to infant death than we have become since the introduction
of vaccines and antibiotics, the demise of a girl of that age, on the
verge of womanhood, must have been hard to bear. But any loss, particularly an abrupt one for which there has been no possible way of

preparing and doing some of the "work of mourning" beforehand, has a way of tainting all experience. Donne's peculiar instrumentality of this random appearance of what we come to realize is the signature line of the poem is remarkable in that the way it figures those aspects of mourning that few writers mention, let alone put to use. I remember reading an analysis of J. D. Salinger's short stories that suggested that most of them describe a person with a wound, and then the question arises as to whether the wound still hurts, and, yes, indeed, it does. Donne's refrain line impends for a long time, and then, when we do get to it, we find that, yes, it still hurts, and there is a kind of satisfaction in that. We are not (yet) unfaithful to the grief we feel. We are still observant members of the cult of death.

Donne has been talking philosophically about the models of the cosmos that used to be thought of as perfect circles but now have been refined and corrected and, of course, turn out to have orbits that are eccentric and imperfect. The metaphor is clear about how our understanding of all things has been refined, while the things themselves have been revealed to be worse than we had supposed, which is entirely characteristic of the "truth" that depression reveals. The force of the lines, however, is magnified by that suspension we are experiencing and by the lines that we are waiting for but that do not appear. And then, there is a hint, a teaser, a line that begins with the word we are expecting:

> She, who if those great Doctors truly said
> That the Ark to man's proportions was made,
> Had been a type for that, as that might be
> A type of her in this, that contrary
> Both elements, and passions lived at peace
> In her, who caused all civil war to cease.
> She, after whom, what form soe'er we see
> Is discord, and rude incongruity;
> She, she is dead, she's dead; when thou know'st this
> Thou know'st how ugly a monster this world is . . .

The arguments are interesting, but their ingeniousness cannot quite conceal the bitterness that prompts them: we read the exposi-

tion and pay attention to it, but we are also mindful of the grief and
rage behind it. Depression, after all, is anger turned inward, and this
catalog of general corruption and ruin functions at least at one level
as symptomatology. It is up there with Juvenal, with Timon's rhetorical spewings, with Swift's manifesto of disgust, and with Pope's
venomous outpourings in *The Dunciad,* so rich and lively as to beguile us into taking it at face value, as commentary on the world—
which it is, but only in part. The hyperbole is what ought to remind
us that the speaker is not altogether in his right mind:

> Sight is the noblest sense of any one,
> Yet sight hath only colour to feed on,
> And colour is decayed: summer's robe grows
> Dusky, and like an oft dyed garment shows.
> Our blushing red, which used in cheeks to spread,
> Is inward sunk, and only our souls are red.
> Perchance the world might have recovered,
> If she whom we lament had not been dead:
> But she, in whom all white, and red, and blue
> (Beauty's ingredients) voluntary grew,
> As in an unvexed paradise; from whom
> Did all things' verdure, and their lustre come,
> Whose composition was miraculous,
> Being all colour, all diaphanous,
> (For air, and fire but thick gross bodies were,
> and liveliest stones but drowsy, and pale to her,)
> She, she, is dead; she's dead: when thou know'st this,
> Thou know'st how wan a ghost this our world is . . .

The final occurrence of the refrain line is another fifty verses on,
in what is therefore the climax of the poem, a wonderfully rueful
consideration of the departed's benign influence on the world,
which, now that she is gone, is also gone:

> She, from whose influence all impressions came,
> But, by receiver's impotencies, lame,
> Who, though she could not transubstantiate

> All states to gold, yet gilded every state,
> So that some princes have some temperance;
> Some counsellors some purpose to advance
> The common profit; and some people have
> Some stay, no more than kings should give, to crave;
> Some women have some taciturnity;
> Some nunneries, some grains of chastity.
> She that did thus much, and much more could do,
> But that our age was iron, and rusty too,
> She, she is dead; she's dead: when thou know'st this,
> Thou know'st how dry a cinder this world is.

And he goes on to say:

> And learn'st thus much by our anatomy,
> That 'tis in vain to dew, or mollify
> It with thy tears, or sweat or blood: nothing
> Is worth our travail, grief, or perishing,
> But those rich joys, which did possess her heart,
> Of which she's now partaker, and a part.

The long poem has pretty much fallen out of the contemporary repertory. It is difficult enough to get a short poem published, but long poems are an embarrassment to poetry editors who know their place and understand the constraints of the magazine business. Those few commercial magazines, such as *Atlantic Monthly* and the *New Yorker,* that publish poetry do so because it provides cheaper and tonier filler than cartoons, but even *Partisan Review* has length limits, which may not be specified but which weigh, nonetheless, on the selection process. To publish even a hundred-line poem is to use up all the space of the issue and infuriate all the poets who have submitted. Poetry editors are in a difficult enough situation, making twenty or fifty or a hundred enemies to whom they send rejections for every friend to whom they can send an acceptance. Meanwhile, in school and college classrooms, poems have become mostly exercises, hoops for students to jump through, and the short poem is pedagogically convenient as a set piece for an essay. For poets, then, the long poem has become that acte gratuit, attractive to a writer only because it is even more inutile than Verlaine could ever have imagined. And for readers, the taste for long poems and even the ability to read them has been compromised. For most of the few who read poetry at all, the short lyric is quick, diverting, not too demanding, and altogether satisfactory.

It was as an exercise, to teach myself something about how to handle the modulations of tone and timbre that enable the long discursive poem, that I began playing with a translation of Virgil's *Georgics*. And of all contemporary poetry, I think Howard Nemerov's work, which people may still read but which nobody seems to talk about much anymore, offered the most valuable model of how to manage a paragraph in verse. That I didn't come back for instruction to Donne's "An Anatomy of the World" seems odd, but I didn't understand the poem, had no idea what it was doing, and couldn't have begun to guess how it worked.

I don't know of any discussions of how it happens—as it often does—that a work of literature holds itself in waiting in this way for the proper moment. Eighteen to twenty-two seems an odd time in life for an encounter with certain works, for which these youngsters cannot possibly be emotionally equipped, however well they have been trained in explication and classroom performance. Even if Madsen and Martz and Nicolson had seen in the poem what I see, and even if they had tried to explain to me what I have had to puzzle out for myself about its unusual strategy, I don't think I could have connected to it the way I do now.

Martz much prefers "Of the Progress of the Soul: The Second Anniversary," which he finds to have "a unity not achieved in the earlier poem." While I can admire this second poem, it does not speak to me as intimately as does the first, but that may be in part because I have never achieved that reintegration of faith and hope and that healing of spirit the second poem describes and, by implication, prescribes. Ordinarily, mourning takes a year, which happens to be the length of time during which Jews say the Kaddish for a deceased parent, or spouse, or child. For "complicated mourning," as is sometimes occasioned by a violent death, twenty years is only a beginning.

Martz's preference for the second poem may, therefore, be an indication of his mental health as much as of his literary taste and critical judgment. But for those of us who are deeply wounded in our hearts, "The First Anniversary" is one of the great comforts in literature—offering reassurance and solace in the depths of the abyss, or at least demonstrating, as it does so well, that others have been there, that others have felt this bitter despair. What it does, dramatically and rhetorically, is truly daring. But Donne, after all, was not merely a great poet but a great churchman, too, who was dean of St. Paul's, and, had he lived, might well have gone on to be the archbishop of Canterbury. He knew what he was about.

Shine in the Dreadfull Dark: The Sidnean Psalms

IT IS PERHAPS HELPFUL, AS mithridate to the frenzies of speculative day trading in the literary marketplace, to consider how leisurely the process can be by which a poet's reputation finds its proper—or at least temporarily settled—level. In the publication last year of *The Collected Works of Mary Sidney Herbert, the Countess of Pembroke*,[1] there is encouragement for those of us who may have been discouraged, depressed, or even at the point of giving up hope altogether. These moving, accomplished, and immediately engaging poems have been waiting since 1621 for this belated and still slightly beclouded admission into the canon.

The delay is, in part, the countess's own fault. While she was assiduous in getting the work of her brother, Sir Philip Sidney, into print—an undertaking that reduced the stigma of publication for other writers—she was less forward about her own work. The trans-

1. *The Collected Works of Mary Sidney Herbert*, edited by Margaret P. Hannay, Noel J. Kinnamon, and Michael G. Brennan (Oxford University Press, 1998).

lation of the Psalms that he had commenced she edited and completed: he did 1 through 43, and hers are 44 to 150. But she was
content to have these circulate in manuscript, and they did, indeed,
circulate to the right people—not only to her immediate circle at
Wilton House in Wiltshire (which included Spenser, Fulke Greville,
and Samuel Daniel), but Queen Elizabeth, who was sent a copy with
an elegant dedicatory poem by the countess. John Donne has a poem,
fifty-six lines long, "Upon the translation of the Psalmes by Sir
Philip and the Countesse of Pembroke his sister," which praises their
work with unalloyed enthusiasm:

> The songs are these, which heavens high holy Muse
> Whisper'd to *David, David* to the Jewes:
> And *Davids* Successors, in holy zeale,
> In formes of joy and art to re-reveale
> To us so sweetly and sincerely too,
> That I must not rejoyce as I would doe
> When I behold that these Psalmes are become
> So well attyr'd abroad, so ill at home,
> So well in Chambers, in thy Church so ill,
> As I can scarce call that reform'd untill
> This be reformed; Would a whole State present
> A lesser gift than some one man hath sent?
> And shall our Church unto our Spouse and King
> More hoarse, more harsh than any other, sing?
> For *that* we pray, we praise thy name for *this,*
> Which, by this *Moses* and this *Miriam,* is
> Already done; and as those Psalmes we call
> (Though some have other Authors) *Davids* all:
> So though some have, some may some Psalmes translate,
> We thy Sydnean Psalms shall celebrate,
> And, till we come th'Extemporall song to sing,
> (Learn'd the first hower, that we see the King,
> Who hath translated those translators) may
> These their sweet learned labors, all the way
> Be as our tuning, that, when hence we part
> We may fall in with them, and sing our part.

I must have been a sophomore when I first read that poem, but I cannot possibly have understood except in the vaguest way what Donne was very clearly talking about—the truly terrible translations of the Psalms that had been published in 1562 and were in use in congregational worship in cathedrals and parish churches throughout the country and that had gone though 150 editions by 1621, the year of the countess's death.

In the introduction to *The Psalms of Sir Philip Sidney and the Countess of Pembroke,* edited by J. C. A. Rathmell and published in 1963, there is a sample of the kind of thing Donne was talking about, a version published in the Anglo-Genevan Psalter of 1556 by John Hopkins of Psalm 55:

> But God shall cast them deep in pit,
>   That thirst for blood always:
> He will no guileful man permit
>   To live out half his days.
> Though such be quite destroid and gone,
>   In thee O Lord I trust:
> I shall depend thy grace upon
>   With all my heart and lust.

Not surprisingly, Donne found this unexciting, both as a poet and as a clergyman. He was, we may remember, dean of St. Paul's and would very probably, except for his failing health, been made a bishop. The countess's version would have appealed to him as literature and also as an occasion for spiritual exploration and cultivation:

> but lord, how long shall these men tarry heere?
> fling them in pitt of death where never shin'd
>   the light of life and while I make my stay
>   on thee, let who their thirst with bloud allay
> have their life-holding threed so weakly twin'd
> that it half spunne, death may in sunder sheare.

George Herbert, another great poet cleric of the seventeenth century and a kinsman of the countess's, would also almost certainly have known the Sidnean Psalms. Indeed, it has been suggested, by Louis Martz among others, that their psalmody was one of the most important influences on his development as a religious poet.

Such overwhelming authority ought to have been enough to establish the countess, but her work remained inaccessible for centuries, largely because of her own lack of enthusiasm about appearing in print. After her death of smallpox in 1621 at age fifty-nine, her wishes were respected with a bizarre scrupulousness. It wasn't until 1823 that the Chiswick Press brought out a smallish edition. And in 1963, as a part of the Doubleday Anchor Seventeenth-Century Series, *The Psalms of Sir Philip Sidney and the Countess of Pembroke* appeared, edited by J. C. A. Rathmell. (It was reissued by New York University Press and is now out of print, but there is a selection of fifty of the countess's psalms and a dozen of Sir Philip's, chosen and with the spelling modernized by R. E. Pritchard, published in 1992 by Carcanet and available in the United States. The forty-four psalms of Sir Philip, then, are available only in Rathmell or in the Ringler edition of Sidney's poems,[2] which is out of print but available from used-book dealers for anywhere between twenty-four and eighty-one dollars.)

Rathmell's 1963 publication ought to have changed the landscape of English studies, but the countess's preferences—or prayers?— were still somehow being heeded. The sixties were not the best decade for such poetry. For one thing, seventeenth-century studies had peaked. Those exegetes and textual analysts who were the scholarly division of new criticism had gone over that ground impressively well, and smart young academics looking to make their own reputations and careers were foraging elsewhere. (Harold Bloom, leading the way, was working on Blake in the early sixties; then, in a demonstration of unrivaled quirky power, he moved on to offer a course bluntly but accurately titled "Bloom on Bloom.")

2. *The Poems of Sir Philip Sidney*, edited by William A. Ringler Jr. (Clarendon Press, 1962).

The campus disturbances of the sixties were not helpful either. To read the countess's psalms aright, one needs a degree of poise and playfulness. Of civility, one might say. And the students then—the graduate students, especially—were too earnest and fervent and dull to qualify as her appropriate audience. The fact that she was female ought to have helped, but feminism, which was just getting underway, had (and still has) its own peculiar agenda. For a writer simply to be a woman was not enough; they were looking for women who were outcasts, whose work, however unpolished and naive, could be a vehicle for the scholars' sense of moral outrage and a way to exact payment for all kinds of wrongs the feminists believed their gender had suffered. (The ideal women's lit subject is perhaps Charlotte Perkins Gilman, whose angry but not very impressive short story, "The Yellow Wallpaper," is the basis of an entire academic industry.) Often, the women's studies people are, like many ecologists, Marxists without Marx, and because they could not condescend to the Countess of Pembroke, who was singularly unneedy, they simply ignored her. Finally, in this Age of Aquarius, the biblical source of the poetry weighed considerably against her. In public schools, these days, the Bible is the new forbidden book.

There was some notice, of course. In his introduction to *The Psalms in English*,[3] the late Donald Davie wrote:

> When in 1981 I edited *The New Oxford Book of Christian Verse*, I tried to stem the tide of oblivion by printing five of the Countess of Pembroke's psalm-versions, proposing for good measure that on the evidence of these compositions the Countess was "the first woman-poet of genius in the history of English poetry." This was designedly a gift to feminist literary criticism. But the gift was spurned.

It was, indeed, and, peculiarly enough, the countess's aristocratic preferences seem still to have retained much of their force. Oxford's recent publication of her collected work, a full-dress two-volume undertaking with complete scholarly apparatus, is so outrageously

---

3. *The Psalms in English*, edited by Donald Davie (Penguin Books, 1996).

expensive as to discourage casual adventuring by any mere amateurs. At best, its appearance may spark some interest in the Pritchard selection of the Sidnean Psalms, but that volume is not altogether satisfactory, being only a sampling, and isn't easy to find. And the intellectual weather remains inhospitable. The latest fad of academic know-nothings involves a bias on the left against translation as a kind of intellectual imperialism, which dovetails nicely with a similar bias on the right, the belief that translation is inevitably a betrayal of the nuanced authenticity of the text in the source language.

The fact remains, however, that the countess was one of the greatest poets of what remains the greatest age of English letters. That she is clearly more accomplished than her more famous brother has probably worked to her disadvantage. Seventeenth-century scholars are like any scholars in that they know what they know and aren't eager for revaluations. They don't read the literature anymore, but the literature on the literature. Sir Philip is graceful and elegant, if a little mannered. Here is his version of Psalm 23:

> The Lord, the Lord my shepheard is,
> > And so can never I
> > > Tast misery,
> He rests me in greene pasture his:
> > By waters still, and sweete
> > > He guides my feete.

> He me revives: leades me the way,
> > Which righteousness doth take,
> > > For his names sake.
> Yea though I should through valleys stray,
> > Of deathes dark shade, I will
> > > Noe whitt feare ill.

> For thou, deere Lord, thou me besett'st:
> > Thy rodd, and thy staff be
> > > To comfort me;

Before me thou a table sett'st,
    Even when foes envious ey
        Doth it espy.

Thou oilst my head, thou fillst my cupp;
    Nay more thou endless good,
        Shalt give me food.
To thee, I say, ascended up,
    Where thou, the Lord of all,
        Dost hold thy hall.

He has a sprightliness and the right pastoral feeling, but his sister's work is even more impressive. Her authority is immediate and incontrovertible. The splendid psalm of praise, the 150th, she renders as:

O laud the Lord, the God of hoasts commend,
    exault his pow'r, advaunce his holynesse:
    with all your might lift his almightinesse:
your greatest praise upon his greatness spend.

Make Trumpetts noise in shrillest notes ascend:
    make Lute and Lyre his loved fame expresse:
    him lett the pipe, hym lett the tabrett blesse,
him Organs breath, that windes or waters lend.

Lett ringing Timbrells soe his honor sound,
    lett sounding Cymballs so his glory ring,
that in their tunes such mellody be found,

As fitts the pompe of most triumphant king.
conclud: by all that aire, or life enfold,
    lett high Jehova highly be extold.

It is a dance of language, with syntactical setups and payoffs, inversions and postponed verbs that syncopate and snap ("him lett the pipe, hym lett the tabrett blesse,") and a playfulness that finds a plausible English equivalent to the sprightliness of the Hebrew.

The dreariness of the prayerbook renditions about which Donne complained arises in part from the different intention of those translators, who are very regular and intend their transcriptions for use as hymns. Without the music, the bareness of Charles Wesley's 150th is painful:

> Praise the Lord who reigns above
> And keeps his court below;
> Praise the holy God of love,
> And all his greatness show;
> Praise him for his noble deeds,
> Praise him for his matchless pow'r
> Him from whom all good proceeds
> Let earth and heav'n adore.
>
> Celebrate th'eternal God
> With harp and psaltery,
> Timbrels soft and cymbals loud
> in his high praise agree.
> Praise him ev'ry tuneful string;
> All the reach of heav'nly art,
> All the pow'rs of music bring,
> The music of the heart.
>
> Him, in whom they move and live,
> Let ev'ry creature sing,
> Glory to their Maker give,
> And homage to their King.
> Hallowed be his name beneath,
> As in heav'n on earth adored;
> Praise the Lord in ev'ry breath,
> Let all things praise the Lord.

It is, to be kind, heavy-footed. That "pow'r" / "adore" rhyme in the first stanza is regrettable, and for the contemporary reader, "The music of the heart" of the second bears the Hallmark hallmark. The timbre of the poem is clearly one that demands a musicality in the prosody, which the countess takes as her warrant for baroque embellishment that she announces in the first nervy flourish, "O laud the Lord." It is the last psalm and, therefore, her valedictory piece, and it is no accident that the form she uses in this virtuoso performance is the Petrarchan sonnet, which her brother had made his own in *Astrophel and Stella.*

Having tried my own hand at some of these poems,[4] I have some sense of the risks of the undertaking. I was somewhat less brash, I'm afraid:

> Hallelujah! Praise God, you
> in his earthly temple. Angels, too,
> in their heavenly congregation, praise
> His might and the justice of His ways.
> Praise Him for what he does and is.
> Praise with the trumpets' fanfares His
> magnificence. With harp and lyre
> praise! In your song and dance, admire
> and praise! With cymbal, snare, and drum,
> with every twangle, flourish and thrum,
> praise Him. And let each living thing
> praise Him with every breath and sing:
>   Hallelujah!

I was well pleased, I must confess, with the effect of that enjambment at the end of the sixth line and the way it throws weight on "magnificence," but it can't begin to compare with the impact of the deferred verb in the countess's fourth line, where "spend" explodes and, in its extraordinary force, reminds us even of its sexual aspect. It is a syntactical equivalent of Bernini's statue of Saint Theresa in her ecstasy.

---

4. *Sixty-One Psalms of David,* translated by David R. Slavitt (Oxford University Press, 1996).

A good number of the Psalms are acrostic, with the Hebrew running down the right-hand margin (Hebrew is read from right to left). This is, at the least, a distraction, which is a legitimate poetic strategy, a way of occupying the left lobe of the reader's brain so that the critical faculties are lulled and the logic of the argument can sneak in and take possession of the spirit. There is also a mystical element at work, the notion that the words are sacred vessels carrying their meanings in ways too complicated and subtle for most of us even to be able to imagine. This acrostic exercise occurs elsewhere in the Bible—the Book of Lamentations has several elaborate performances in poetry that is not at all playful but, on the contrary, full of the deepest grief in literature. Most translators ignore these tropes as an irrelevance or even an embarrassment. The countess, not so easily flustered, recognized that there can be, in a *jeu d'esprit*, real spirit. Her Psalm 117 is praise of the Lord that announces that down the left-hand majuscules:

> P raise him that ay
> R emains the same:
> A ll tongues display
> I ehovas fame.
> S ing all that share
> T his earthly ball:
> H is mercies are
> E xpos'd to all.
> L ike as the word
> O nce he doth give,
> R old in record,
> D oth time outlyve.

This kind of playfulness might seem to have little to do with spirituality, but here Davie is quite correct in his insistence that

> what looks like vaunting is really apprehensive humility. The poems that she makes out of the Psalms are gifts that she lays on the altar; and she is at pains to show that her gifts are as "costly" as those that the Magi brought to the Christ-child in Bethlehem.

Their brilliance, their variety, their dexterity are pressed on our attention to persuade us that anything less would fail to meet the awe-inducing occasion. To say it again, the entire enterprise is a work of devotion; it glorifies God by heaping up before Him all the glories it can muster. The versifier has one gift, that of versifying: and that gift, the only one he or she has, is laid before the Throne. This is a motive that, one may suppose and hope, impels certain poets in this as in previous centuries.

The imputation of motive is risky, always. There can be no question that, in large measure, piety and her love for her brother were what moved the countess to undertake the work, but along with such high-mindedness came such basic satisfactions as that of doing a difficult thing well. Pritchard seems quite persuasive when he suggests that she

> might have felt uneasy about seeking to "match the matchless unicorn," her celebrated brother, but there would have been some inhibition about the very act of writing, as a woman. At that time women were strongly discouraged from any public self-assertion or literary activity. Her parade of poetic skill might be partly an indication of female capability, partly also an expression—particularly through any forced phrasing—of the tension produced by this act of presumption. In Petrarch's *Rime* or Philip's *Astrophel and Stella*, the protagonist adopts a variety of roles: so too does the speaker of the psalms (Philip remarked on David's "often and free changing of persons"), speaking variously as prophet, king, or anguished private individual. If the Countess, as Elizabethan lady, could not easily speak out publicly, she could at least, as a mouthpiece of the Psalmist's (male) voices, and like Shakespeare's heroines, speak most for herself when speaking as another.

Or, to put it a slightly different way, there are some constraints that are enabling and empowering. Privileged though she may have been, she was mortal, afflicted, and by no means immune from grief. In

1586, both her parents died, and then her brother Philip, wounded in
the Low Countries at Zutphen, developed gangrene and died, too.
The translation of the Psalms allowed her to express the emotion she
must have felt. This is her version of the agonized Psalm 88:

> My god, my lord, my help, my health;
>> to thee my cry
>> doth restles fly.
>> both when of sunn the day
>> the treasures doth display,
> and night locks up his golden wealth.
>
> Admitt to presence what I crave:
>> ô bow thine eare
>> my cry to heare,
>> whose soule with ills and woes
>> soe flowes, soe overflowes,
> that now my life drawes nigh the grave.
>
> with them that fall into the pitt
>> I stand esteem'd:
>> quite forcelesse deem'd,
>> as one who free from strife,
>> and sturr of mortall life,
> among the dead at rest doth sitt.
>
> Right like unto the murdred sort,
>> who in the grave
>> their biding have:
>> whom now thou dost no more
>> remember as before,
> quite, quite cut off from thy support.
>
> Throwne downe into the grave of graves
>> in darknes deepe
>> thou do'st me keepe:

where lightning of thy wrath
upon me lighted hath,
all overwhelm'd with all thy waves.

Who did know me, whom I did know,
remov'd by thee
are gone from me
are gone? that is the best:
they all me so detest,
that now abrode I blush to goe.

My wasted ey doth melt away
fleeting amaine,
in streames of paine
while I my praiers send,
while I my hands extend,
to thee, my god, and faile noe day.

Alas, my lord, will then be tyme,
when men are dead,
thy truth to spread?
shall they, whome death hath slaine,
to praise thee live againe,
and from their lowly lodgings clime?

Shall buried mouthes thy mercies tell?
dust and decay
thy truth display?
and shall thy workes of mark
shine in the dreadfull dark?
thy Justice where oblivions dwell?

Good reason then I cry to thee,
and ere the light
salute thy sight,
my plaint to thee direct.

lord, why dost thou reject
my soule, and hide thy face from me?

Ay me, alas, I faint, I dy,
    so still, so still
      thou dost me fill,
    and hast from yongest yeares,
    with terrifying feares,
that I, in traunce, amaz'd doe ly.

All over me thy furies past:
    thy feares my mind
    doe fretting bind
    flowing about mee soe,
    as flocking waters flow:
no day can overrun their haste.

Who erst to me were neare and deare
    farr now, ô farr
    disjoyned ar:
    and when I would them see,
    who my acquaintance be,
as darknesse they to me appeare.

Harold Bloom
and the Decline
of Civility

I HAVE MET HAROLD BLOOM only once. It was in 1956, at a
dinner for Scholars of the House—a cosseted bunch of undergraduate Yalies who, for their senior year, were excused from all classes,
exams, and academic appointments, given "the freedom of the university," and asked to do only four things. We were, during that year,
to write an academic or creative book (or make a film, or something
on that scale), sit for an oral exam at the end of the year, meet more
or less regularly with a member of the faculty who was our tutor and
adviser, and come to dinner every other Wednesday evening to join
the other scholars and those members of the Yale faculty who were
interested in what we were doing.

This program was abandoned some years ago. My daughter's
theory is that at sixteen hundred dollars a year—which is what Yale
cost, including room and board, when I was there—the Scholar of
the House program was not inherently absurd. When those annual
room, board, and tuition charges passed twenty thousand dollars, the
idea of just hanging around without taking any courses began to

seem somewhat self-indulgent. More paranoid than she is, I took the termination of the program as a sign of waning health of the Yale community. The Scholar of the House program was a strange hot-house flower, depending for its survival on faculty members like Richard Sewall and Paul Weiss and a few others who were so secure in their eminence that they could afford to be interested in education. That program had started after World War II, when the returning veterans made Yale the most exciting place it has been, probably, in its history. It continued because professors cared about the students, the dozen or so best and most independent of each class of about a thousand.

I had a brief correspondence about its demise with Benno Schmidt, who was president of Yale at the time, and he denied that the university had in any way undercut or sabotaged the program. But I never entirely believed him. I thought, and still think, that they'd lost their nerve when they limited it to people who had already completed the requirements for a departmental major—so they wouldn't have to flunk anyone who didn't do well, gambling with a fourth of his undergraduate career and losing. This meant that the restless and the liveliest young men—we were all young men, then—who had learned the techniques for doing the work of a fourteen-week course and were bored by that weren't candidates anymore. They had now limited themselves to those grinds and advanced-placement students who had nearly managed to graduate at the end of their junior year, and for these there were other temptations. They could, for instance, devote that fourth year to graduate study and earn an MA along with the BA in their four years—an attractive option.

But my sense is, still, that if the ethos had remained what it was, collegial as well as collegiate, the heavyweight professors would have continued to support the program. It may have been a bit breezy and amateurish, but it taught us about the uses of freedom. I was lucky to have been part of it and luckier still to have had a life and a career for which that year was such a relevant period of training. The Yale faculty seemed in the sixties and seventies to be turning careerist, asserting themselves in ways that were quite novel. They weren't like the professors I remembered, but a bunch of hustlers.

And for such people, the departments are where the money is and where the goodies come from. These general programs of the college can't do a damned thing for the faculty, and the faculty seems not to have exercised themselves to do much for them.

What led me to this dour view was the change in the culture that took place particularly in the English department at Yale. It was, when I was there in the middle fifties, a gentlemanly place. There was a series of classes, of course, but the undertaking went beyond that to include the Yale amenities of lunches in the dining halls of residential colleges, where the faculty fellows could eat for free if they were willing to socialize with the undergraduates. There were the lounges and seminar rooms in the various colleges where we sprawled on leather couches and where our classes looked and felt like conversations about literature. And there was the Elizabethan Club—a house, an endowed teapot, and a small fortune's worth of Elizabethan books in a vault, because William Lyon Phelps thought it would be a fine idea to encourage good conversation, which he associated with good books and a cup of tea. He got Alexander Smith Cochran, heir to the Yonkers carpet fortune, to set up the club and give his books to it. It is a wifty and peculiarly Yaleish institution, and I remember it with fondness. One can, indeed, pursue the ideals of learning and civility more easily over a plate of cucumber sandwiches than in any classroom. And these dinners of the Scholars of the House were a similar manifestation of what I took to be Yale's self-confidence, its assurance that, even if only by osmosis, a bright group of young men would inevitably learn from a gifted, distinguished, and caring community of scholars and writers.

It was at one of those dinners that I was introduced to Harold Bloom—I think by Cleanth Brooks, who had been one of my teachers the year before. Cleanth was a short, neat, very southern, very witty man with a remarkable gift for dry understatement. Bloom was large, louder, wearing what I remember vividly as a deplorable tie— I think in need of cleaning.

(His tie? Is that a legitimate subject for criticism? But then, if not, why not? A tie, after all, is as much a piece of iconography and an expression of taste as anything else. A tie is a statement, a part of one's style, as much as one's prose surely. And this was clearly a complicated assertion of grudging compliance, a yielding to the Yale standards of gentlemanliness that managed at the same time to defy them, or at the least to withhold any personal endorsement.)

He was, at the time, a graduate student and teaching assistant. I asked him what he was working on.

"Shelley," he barked.

I behaved badly, I'm afraid. He was the most un-Shelleyan looking guy I had ever seen in my life. Curly Howard would have been a likelier enthusiast of the *Epipsychidion*. I laughed aloud, I am ashamed to say. Bloom looked hurt—he had the soulful eyes of a basset hound and they still have a baleful look to them.

I shouldn't have laughed like that and I apologize. But I was not altogether wrong to have noticed a certain dissonance, which was what had prompted my rudeness, after all. I didn't make any awful jokes, didn't point out, for instance, that Shelley, Byron, and Milton were not a bunch of Jewish druggists but dead British writers, even though it might well have crossed my mind to do so.

Forty years later, I still see the humor but I see the macabre side of it, too. For one thing, Harold Bloom has gone on to be a big gun himself, just as much a heavyweight as Richard Sewall and William Wimsatt and Cleanth Brooks and Robert Penn Warren were in 1956. But the study of English is not what it was. It has turned nasty and brutish, and Bloom is the man who is in large part responsible for this. And I suspect he knows it, and that is why his eyes have that baleful and almost haunted look.

I don't blame him. In some ways, I find his intelligence admirably keen and I think he saw even more clearly what I had roughly perceived—that if Yale in the fifties was a paradise of New Criticism, it was largely because Brooks and Warren were there. And the New Criticism is interesting because it was so markedly a southern enterprise: Brooks, Warren, Tate, Ransom, and those others were all southerners and they all shared a tradition in which fundamentalist fervor for scripture was a lively impulse, and rhetoric—in the courthouse and at the pulpit—was a living art. If you take that passion for the word and secularize it, what you get is *Understanding Poetry*, the Brooks and Warren text that set the standard for analysis and discussion of poems for an entire generation.

Bloom realized that, as a Jew, he had an even grander hermeneutic tradition of midrash and Talmudic pilpul on which to draw, and that if he took this apparatus and applied it to those Romantic poets for whom the instruments of New Criticism had been least successful, he might make a career for himself. He seized, therefore, upon Shelley, and then, quite soon thereafter, Blake, with whom he made his reputation.

Better yet, you don't have to read these writers so much as subdue them. It was pilpul, but with a little Kabbalah and a lot of Freud in it, and in the seventies Bloom adopted the notion of influence that Walter Jackson Bate had introduced in *The Burden of the Past and the English Poets*. (Bloom's central book, *The Anxiety of Influence,* came out in 1973.)

So far, I admire him, or, more candidly, I have mixed feelings in which admiration preponderates. That kind of strategic thinking is, in itself, broader and more interesting than most of what English scholars produce in their careers. It was a new way of reading, which is always interesting. But it is better at second hand. I have never liked reading Bloom himself because he writes badly. His sentences are bristling and ugly. He shows off. He bullies. He is ruder to his readers than I was to him. Either that or, what's worse in a critic, he has no taste. Or he flaunts bad taste, bludgeoning us with it—as he did with that tie.

Here is a bit, chosen at random, from *Figures of Capable Imagination*. Actually, I'm giving Bloom something of a break here, because this is a passage about Geoffrey Hill, a poet whom I much admire and whom I read with careful attention. Hill's work is difficult and it deserves and repays the kind of intellectual scrutiny that is Bloom's forte. He cites a passage from "Annunciations" and says of it:

> This is again a Gnostic sublimity. Blake could still insist that pity survived only because we kept on rendering others piteous, but Hill comes later, and for him the intoxication of belatedness is to know that our reality and our desire are both negated by our appearance as legatees. It is a tradition that makes us into "contractual ghosts of pity." A Beautiful Necessity prepossesses us, and

makes us bear witness to a dead but still powerful transcendence. Hill characterizes one of his sequences as "a florid grim music" or an "ornate and heartless music punctuated by mutterings, blasphemies and cries for help." A baroque pathos seems to be Hill's goal with the ornateness his tribute to tradition, and the punctuation of pathos his outcry against tradition. Hill's is clearly a poetics of pain, in which all the calamities of history become so many poetic salutes, so many baroque meditations, always trapped in a single repetition of realization. (241)

What? My mind wanders. How is pathos baroque? Can calamities become salutes? I can't help but feel assaulted.

I must also confess I was a little ashamed of myself back then. I didn't want to seem, even to myself, like some anti-Semitic Jew. (The issue is uncomfortable, but it comes up whenever one Jew thinks that another, asserting his Jewishness as an integral part of his identity, is behaving badly. One doubts one's own right to disapprove. It wasn't until I came across John Murray Cuddihy's book *The Ordeal of Civility* that I was able at last to arrive at a tolerable accommodation. Cuddihy talks in an interesting and nearly obsessive way about Jews coming late into the secular society and how we are therefore people who are likely to say the unsayable. Marx talks about money, and Freud talks about sex, both of which subjects used to be taboo in respectable nineteenth-century drawing rooms or salons. I hope Professor Bloom will understand that I mean it at least in part as a compliment when I suggest that he, too, and in a peculiarly Jewish way, has been saying one of the things that, at least in the fifties, was still unsayable—that in some fundamental aspect, most intellectual work turns out to be a pissing contest.

We all know this, although we may be reluctant to admit it. There is something wonderfully satisfying about being brilliantly right, and nothing demonstrates one's rightness more dramatically than the crestfallen look of the adversary who has to admit that he or she is *wrong*. That is why courtroom dramas are so appealing. We love the moment when the barrister adjusts his wig, flashes a wintry smile, and then says, with ringing plosives and sibilants, "I put it to you, sir, that your entire testimony is a tissue of lies."

In Yale's mix, in the fifties, there were other flavors and ingredients in the departmental soup. William Wimsatt, author of *The Verbal Icon*, was an Aristotelian who had taken the machinery of Aristotle's *Politics* and applied it to literary theory, asking whether the poem was what the poet intended, what the reader perceived, or some third thing. Bloom took up that kind of thinking, which was congenial to him and fit nicely into his method. What strikes me as remarkable about Bloom's criticism is that the subject is always elsewhere. Blake is struggling with Milton, who is wrestling with Shakespeare, who is confronting Chaucer, who engages with Boccaccio, and so on back until we get Pindar sparring with Homer. We start with the words on the page, but we soon move to a discussion of their psychic significance, how they assert or modify a "self," and, by the way, we turn ourselves from readers and participants into referees in an endless scrum.

Bloom claims that he is paying scrupulous attention to the works at hand and he disapproves of those who have followed his own lead, exhibiting what he calls "a critical preference for context over text" because they are "a generation made impatient with deep reading." But he was the one who opened the door. His concerns about influence are not textual but intertextual and contextual.

The question of influence is not useless and can yield a series of interesting observations. Gregory Nagy's remarkable book *Pindar's Homer* is a punctilious working out of Bloom's proposition. But the agon that Bloom sees at the heart of the literary tradition is, at the very least, distracting. To read Milton, it is probably a good idea to have read Shakespeare, and Dante and Virgil, and Cicero too, for that matter. But the questions of sources and influences used to be secondary to the study of the work itself, until Bloom, reversing that arrangement, made the study of influence paramount.

From the purely practical and pedagogical perspective, this seems to me a counterintuitive and even weird thing to do, unless we assume that Bloom was expecting to train up classrooms full of young Miltons, who would need to know this stuff in order to write their own versions of *Paradise Lost*. There are other, more plausible if rather less attractive motives, though, that one might adduce. Bloom's praxis involves a reordering of the usual priorities in which the critic's performance becomes paramount and actually displaces that of the author. In this critic's circus, Bloom can now dispense with the old-fashioned kind of deference teachers used to have for their subjects and be, himself, the ringmaster. He is Childe Harold! Or, no, I think of him rather as dressed up in a white coat as Dr. Bloom, presiding in front of the lecture hall, while the poet lies on the narrow couch of the analyst, a kind of pedagogical exhibit.

And if the students argue or object? Bloom has an answer for them, too—that a strong misreading is the equivalent of a new poem! Milton is now up for grabs: there's Bloom's version, and yours and mine. Playing havoc with Pound's second Canto, we may now say, "Hang it all, Sordello, there are as many Robert Brownings as there are readers of Browning." And they're fighting, each against all, in a sordid Australian tag-team psychomachy of mud-wrestling dwarfs.

The appalling thing is that this representation of the world of scholarship and criticism is not altogether false. It can be this way, and too often it is. Bloom's disturbing notion is that this is how it *ought* to be. He has invented an intellectual Darwinism in which only the strongest survive.

Once we abandon the constraints of modesty and civility as hypocritical and irrelevant, the notion of fidelity to a text is inherently unexciting. The game changes and the real question is how great an outrage a critic can commit upon a text and get away with it. Bloom supposes that Milton was anxious about Shakespeare and Dante, but how about the modern reader who is anxious about Shakespeare, Dante, or any writer who uses sentences longer than those of Kurt Vonnegut? And what if one's grievances aren't just psychic but social and political? Then anxiety becomes resentment, and whoever feels aggrieved by the traditional menu of Chaucer, Spenser, Shakespeare, Milton, Dryden, Pope, Wordsworth, and Eliot can now claim justification for revising the curriculum to suit himself. Or herself. The work of writers who have been traditionally held in high esteem can also be revised—deconstructed and transmogrified—so that there are now articles about anal rape in Jane Austen.

The way to assert "authority" is at the expense of an author. This may make for amusing sessions of the Modern Language Association meetings, but the posture is a strange one in which to be teaching young men and women how to read and inviting them to share in the ownership of the great works of their culture. The gays and lesbians, the Hispanics, the blacks, the feminists, the neo-Marxists, and various other special hyphenated interest groups of whom Bloom vigorously disapproves are all convinced that they are doing Good Works as they assault the curriculum for partisan reasons—and why shouldn't they? Bloom lumps these advocates of social betterment together in what he calls "The School of Resentment." Among these he would include "Lacanians, deconstructionists, Foucault-inspired New Historicists, semioticians, neo-Marxists, and latest model feminists." He is right to feel some annoyance. Yale's inability to figure out a way to spend Lee M. Bass's twenty million dollars on a Western civilization curriculum is amazing, and the university's return of the money, with interest, to Mr. Bass is astonishing.[1] Yale, after all, knows as much as any other institution about fungibility of funds. This is clearly political and nuts. Bloom finds it shocking, I should expect, even though he was the one who, in large measure, enabled the behaviors of these complainers and revisionists.

My own sense is that these meliorists ought to be in political science, or maybe the anthropology department, or even the school of theology, rather than in English, which they find so uncongenial. But it never occurs to them to leave. They claim a "right" to be there. They just want to redecorate and make it more comfortable. They think it is quite wonderful that they even deign sometimes to assign works of those old collaborationists of colonialism, sexism, and oppression.

If Bloom were a moron or a villain, he'd have been unmoved by this sorry spectacle. But I think he is now depressed and offended, and that is why he has written *The Western Canon*. Having begun his career by chopping a hole in the bottom of the boat, he is now alarmed that the water is up to the gunwales and wants to stop the process.

1. Yale's version of the rejection of the money is that Bass wanted the right of approval of the teachers in the program. But the class of 1937 offered the same twenty million without strings, and their offer was rejected also.

He isn't single-handedly responsible for having wrecked the culture of English, after all. There were other great processes underway, tendencies in the zeitgeist that cooperated with him. The vulgarization of campuses that began with the GI Bill and was exacerbated during the Vietnam War provided just the right kind of ecology in which Bloomism could flower. People who had no business in college and never much liked reading found themselves required to go, and they majored in English, because, let's face it, it's easy. All they do is read stories and poems that were written in their native language and were intended to be entertaining and accessible.

These nonstudents, or even antistudents, resented the more difficult writers they were assigned, those old guys who wrote with feathers and used dependent clauses. They weren't going to put up with old-fashioned "appreciation," which seemed as absurd as . . . wearing a jacket and tie to class. Instead of a bad tie, a joke tie, a tie "in quotes," there was the more aggressive look of the open-collared denim shirt and work boots. (The only physical work most of these youngsters have ever done is to break in the boots.)

The heroes of criticism were not explicators of literature so much as they were sappers and saboteurs. David Lehman has written in *Signs of the Times* about the Paul de Man debacle at Yale—a former writer of Nazi collaborationist articles in occupied Belgium who came to Yale and preached the gospel of "deconstruction"—which happens to separate the writer from his text and to scramble the meanings of even the plainest words into unintelligibility. This vogue for obfuscation was bizarre in an institution that had professed on its shield a commitment to *lux* and *veritas*, but Yale was hardly alone. In other institutions there were manifestations of the same kind of fatigue with demanding standards of reasonableness, clarity, measure, and order that had prevailed in the fifties. Jacques Derrida's intellectual nihilism was the glamorous French import that could excuse any disregard for a decorum that was bourgeois and his real target all along. Stanley Fish, vulgarizing Derrida a little (there wasn't much room to go in that direction), came up with "reception theory," which means, essentially, that there isn't any text anymore and that a poem or play or novel is pretty much whatever we think it is.

Bloom's version of this Visigoth notion was even cleverer in its opportunism: he limited the "we" to mean the members of the English department, who in his system "own" literature. Or, actually, when you come right down to it, what he really meant was that he owns it, himself. For a time, he was offering "Bloom on Bloom" as a course at Yale, and students enrolled in it.

The publication of *The Western Canon* may also be an assertion of that fundamental contrariness on which Professor Bloom has based his whole career. The only gesture that remains in which he can be shocking and radical is his proposal of that very regimen of Chaucer, Spenser, Shakespeare, Milton, Dryden, Pope, Wordsworth, and Eliot that was on offer back when I was an undergraduate in the fifties. There are differences in approach, of course. Our enthusiasm for these poets was like that of the baseball fans who go out to the field to watch the game; Bloom's concerns are more closely allied with those of the dealers in trading cards. He pays attention to the game only as much as is necessary for speculating in reputations, personalities, and influences. Denis Donoghue, pointing out in his review in the *TLS* that there is a "multiplicity of misquotations that disfigure *The Western Canon*," observed quite correctly that in Bloom's criticism, there is no show of interest at all, "in literary form, structure, questions of narrative, style, or tone, the fellowship of word and word, syllable and syllable." His view was that "If one is a literary psychologist, the verbal detail doesn't matter much; one quickly translates the words on a page into an approximate gesture of the self, and discusses that instead of the words." He is being, if anything, too kind. My belief is that Bloom is utterly tone deaf. Otherwise, he couldn't write the bristling jargon he enjoys inflicting on us.

Indeed, now that I think of it, I recall that the only defect of Cleanth Brooks's criticism that ever troubled me was his failure ever to remark on the music of a poem. He was more interested in structural ironies and such rhetorical strategies than in the subtleties of performance. Bloom, however much he may be in rebellion against Brooks's Yale, makes exactly the same error, but he makes it bigger. Brooks's prose was at least lucid and inoffensive. Bloom's is so exaggerated as to seem like one more expression of psychic hostility. The message of every page and every paragraph is plain: you want to know what I think? Rub your eyes along these emery board sentences of mine, and, if you get anything whatever out of what I've written, congratulations! But it will have cost you, and I still will have won.

It's a pissing contest, again, with Bloom asserting himself as the *fons et origo.* And the rules in Bloom's arena are very harsh. It is not a great triumph, after all, to persuade someone of a proposition that is self-evident in the first place. To say that "The Rape of the Lock" is a good poem, or that *The Iliad* is interesting and rich, is not to stake a claim in virgin territory. The point is rather to make claims that are not self-evident, not even reasonable, or close to lunacy even, and force them down the retching throat of a meek and accepting audience. So, in *The Western Canon,* he offers Tolstoy's *Hadji Murad* as "my personal touchstone for the sublime in prose fiction, to me the best story in the world, or at least the best that I have ever read."

Hadji Murad is a book I happened not to have read. Indeed, I suspect that it was Bloom's plan that many of the readers of *The Western Canon* (or browsers through it, who far outnumber actual readers) would be unfamiliar with *Hadji Murad,* too. So off I went to the library to get a copy, and . . . it's dreadful. It's a dopey book of Chechen war stories that not even the headlines about the continuing fighting in that region could make interesting. It's virtually a comic book, and the translation is into stiff neo-Victorian English. The book was so bad that I went back to take another look at *Tales of Army Life,* Tolstoy's early writing about the same subject, which I remembered as being quite good. I was startled to see how well it had held up. If anything, it was better than what I'd remembered, or I was better able to see how good it was, how absolutely brilliant. This was where Hemingway learned how to write about soldiering.

It was breathtaking, but wasn't suitable for Bloom's purposes. He concedes that *The Death of Ivan Ilyich, The Kreutzer Sonata, Master and Man,* and *Father Sergius* are all very good. But people have read those books and it wouldn't be startling or original to hold any of them up as "my personal touchstone for the sublime." If one is determined to be in-your-face brilliant, then it has to be with some off-the-wall title most of your colleagues have never even heard of, let alone read. What are they going to do? Admit their ignorance? Lie and claim to have read the book? Go out and read it and then try to argue later? Bloom can consider any of those outcomes as a victory.

Victory is the objective of warfare, and Bloom's peculiar description of the tradition of Western literature is that the entire enterprise is a series of psychic battles: the struggles of poets, playwrights, and novelists against their predecessors' accomplishments and their own sense of "belatedness." Even if one accepts this strange characterization, it might seem that critics, if they play any part in these encounters, are only linesmen and referees. But, no, that's not enough. Bloom sees himself more as a manager. The writers are mere players, and *The Western Canon* is a roster that he offers in deliberate Stengelese.

What made his book successful—a Book-of-the-Month Club selection, even—is not so much the series of twenty-six essays on the canonical writers as the list at the end. Americans love lists, and this offering is merely the latest venture in our long tradition of self-improvement that goes back through Mortimer Adler's Great Books, the Harvard Five-Foot Shelf, and Copeland's Treasury. The assumption of all these enterprises is that books are somehow "good for you." They are the keys that open the golden door to success, wisdom, happiness, contentment, or whatever. One need not be utterly cynical to see these ventures as occasions in which hustlers can repackage texts in the public domain for an audience that will probably never read more than a few pages in one or two randomly selected volumes. The books stand on living-room shelves as prominent icons, trophies, or, say, monuments to salesmanship and the lofty aspirations of middle-class households.

Bloom is operating just a rung or two above these projects, however, for he is defending the idea of the canon as well as writing his prescription about what should be in it. He is letting us know what is on the exam. This is what you have to have read to get into heaven. Those who haven't read these writers or are so brazen and shameless as to admit that they don't intend to, he dismisses as "rabblement."

This is not the best starting place for a study of literature, and it's a deplorable one in which to find oneself at the end of such a journey. Its posture is overbearing to the point of thuggishness, and it misses the point, which remains, at one level or another, pleasure. Love. Delight. Amusement. Generosity. Fun.

There are writers on Bloom's list who are not at all intimidating but are nonetheless endearing. Herrick, for instance, is there. But Bloom has nothing to say about him. What could he say? How can one be aggressive with such a poet? Bloom's aggressiveness I see as a sign of defensiveness against the possible attacks of others (like me, for instance). If he could relax and display a little assurance, an ease, a modesty, and a willingness to admit to quirkiness, I would trust him more when he issues judgments and bestows his approval. I want to know writers of whom—or, better, books of which—he is merely fond. What does he think of Brigid Brophy's *Palace without Chairs* or Ronald Firbank's *Concerning the Eccentricities of Cardinal Pirelli*? He lists Lewis Carroll's "Complete Works" as canonical, but that only makes me wonder whether he has ever actually waded through *Sylvie and Bruno,* a mawkish and deplorable piece. He puts Byron's *Don Juan* up there on the roster, but I find it hard to imagine him laughing aloud, as that poem so often requires. He admits that, personally, he dislikes Philip Larkin and Robert Lowell but lists them anyway, because so many other critics do—and then he covers himself by admitting how it isn't critics but other writers who actually create the canon by their process of reacting to earlier work.

His representation of the act of reading is cockeyed from the start. The very notion of objective value is dangerously abstract and therefore misleading. Value to whom? And when? I have always thought that college students, undergraduates and many graduate students as well, are too young for certain works. At twenty, what do they know about the rhythms of a life? If only a decade ago, they were ten-year-olds, what idea can they have of how people grow and change over time? What sense will they make even of a relatively straightforward novel like Arnold Bennett's *Old Wives' Tale*? My conviction is that those who read Proust too soon—before they are thirty, say—are not only missing most of it but are ruining their chances of coming on it when they are ripe for it and can read it fresh, for the first time.

Professors tend to ignore how young their students are, because in some way it vexes or embarrasses them. Bloom's obliviousness to the naïveté of his students may be different, though, in that his intellectual triumphs diminish in importance if his antagonists are only a gaggle of not particularly sophisticated or well-read kids. His bullying classroom habits are not easy to put aside, however, and addressing us common readers he can be abruptly confrontational. I cannot otherwise explain why he would write: "My late friend Paul de Man liked to analogize the solitude of each literary text and each human death, an analogy I once protested. I had suggested to him that the more ironic trope would be to analogize each human birth to the coming into being of a poem, an analogy that would connect texts as infants are connected, voicelessness linked to past voices, inability to speak linked to what had been spoken to, as all of us have been spoken to, by the dead. I did not win that critical argument because I could not persuade him of the larger human analogue; he preferred the dialectical authority of the more Heideggerian irony."

This is pure Bloomishness, graceless, pretentious, and absurd. The "dialectical authority of the more Heideggerian irony" is academic babble that would be silly except for what it conceals. Heidegger? Heidegger?

Listen, Harold, at that Scholar of the House dinner in the fifties where we met, Paul Weiss, my tutor, was among those present. He is a philosopher who trained with Alfred North Whitehead, but, more to the point, then went off to Germany and studied with Heidegger. Weiss understood right away what is clear to most philosophers and ought to be apparent to all Jews, even though you don't see it—that Heidegger was a Nazi!

So, indeed, was your "late friend Paul de Man," who therefore was not just an "analogist" but a big fan of human death, a connoisseur, even. You were not able to win "that critical argument" because, in the intricacy of the engagement, you neglected to call him a fucking collaborator, slap his face, and then do your best to see that he got fired. Even now, years after he has been revealed as Yale's greatest disgrace of its three centuries, you are showing . . . what? That you are a noble guy, unswerving in your loyalty? That you are so Olympian as to be unmoved by the "criticisms" that have been leveled against de Man?

I don't get it, but I am fairly sure that the dropping of this name is an act of defiance, a show of Bloom's refusal to be intimidated by mere evidence, a digging in of his heels in a desperate attempt to avoid being proven wrong.

I offer one more demonstration, somewhat less spectacular, of Bloom's characteristically bellicose gestures. He writes: "Professor Frank Lentricchia, apostle of social change through academic ideology, has managed to read Wallace Stevens's 'Anecdote of the Jar' as a political poem, one that voices the program of the dominant social class. The art of placing a jar was, for Stevens, allied to the art of flower arranging, and I don't see why Lentricchia should not publish a modest volume on the politics of flower arranging, under the title *Ariel and the Flowers of Our Climate*."

What this is, actually, is a kind of compliment. Lentricchia, a professor at Duke—where he swam in the tank with Stanley, the big Fish—has been called the Dirty Harry of American criticism. He is reportedly proud of the glamour of that sobriquet. We also have to know that, in 1977, in *Wallace Stevens: The Poems of Our Climate,* Bloom staked a particular claim to Stevens. In the strange environment these people have imagined and brought into being, Stevens is a part of Bloom's territory. Anyone who ventures to tread on his turf with a different reading has to be—like Bloom, or like Helen Vendler—a heavyweight. Bloom may not be offering Lentricchia a hearty welcome, but there is an acknowledgment: even to be singled out for insult in a book like this is to be recognized and therefore, in a way, honored.

The decorum here, or the lack of it, is strange to me. Whether Bloom and his colleagues are right or wrong is beside the point. Noah Porter, a president of Yale in the nineteenth century, thought that the teaching of science was a terrible idea because it would tend to undermine the faith of the young gentlemen who were in his charge. He was wrong, but Yale survived. I wonder whether it will survive Bloom. What faith remains is no longer theological, but until recently there used to be a belief in a kind of disenchanted gentle-manliness. "Humane letters" was not an oxymoron. Now, the behavior is that of some street gang with turf wars, insults, and assaults that are exciting, perhaps, but give the youngsters a seriously distorted and diminished idea of what the intellectual and literary life can be.

Robert Penn
Warren

ALTHOUGH I WAS NEVER FORMALLY enrolled in any class he taught, Robert Penn Warren was one of my teachers at Yale. A Scholar of the House in my senior year, I enjoyed what they called the "freedom of the university," so that I was excused from all courses and examinations but allowed to sit in on any classes I chose, with the permission of the instructor of course. The only class I attended regularly was Robert Penn Warren's English 73A, a creative-writing course in prose fiction, which met once a week, in a Silliman College common room in which a dozen or so of us would sprawl on the green leather sofas while Professor Warren read aloud the short stories from *Understanding Fiction* and then, without pretense of any kind, asked us the questions that were printed in the textbook he and Cleanth Brooks had written.

It was a weird experience, and I went because . . . well, first of all, because he was famous. Paul Weiss, the philosopher, who was my Scholar of the House adviser, had once startled me by saying that the subject matter of courses was unimportant and what I should be interested in was studying with "great men." I have come to realize that this is a profound truth and it is advice I gave all my children when they went off to college. Most of the stuff on the course syllabus will leach away, but the style of the man or woman and the demonstration of how a life can include or accommodate to artistic or intellectual work is a lesson that will stay with you always.

If Warren's fame was what brought me in for the first class, his almost courtly charm and his practice of reading aloud were what kept me coming back: I liked being read to. It was cozy and relaxed, and, over the course of the term, it developed into a demonstration that much of what passes for literary criticism is irrelevant and unnecessary. What counts is the text itself, and you can learn a lot about a literary work and communicate a lot, too, to students just by reading it aloud. There may be places you want to stop and make a remark—I do believe in remarks, which tend to be specific and therefore helpful—but I don't remember Warren doing that often. The process of reading aloud in a group is as different from solitary silent reading as communal prayer in a congregation is different from individual devotion.

It was a breezy, even a cheeky thing for Warren to be doing, and what it suggested was in an odd way consonant with what Weiss had said—the class wasn't important. The work of the course, anyway, was what each of us would do on his own, writing the stories Professor Warren would read, and then the crucial encounter would be with him, alone, in his office, where he'd go over what we'd done, explaining what worked and what didn't, or, sometimes, suggesting what might be fixed to work better. This was intimate and also authoritative—not only because he was who he was but also because this is how I'd learned from Dudley Fitts, my teacher at Andover, that this should be done. Warren's judgments were sometimes different from Fitts's but their method was much the same.

The department, the registrar, and the dean believed in classes, so Warren couldn't altogether dispense with them without risking a fight he didn't need. This story hour of his was his way of holding a class without holding a class, of meeting with us for three hours a week and fulfilling the administration's requirements. That, too, was an important and valuable lesson. What you learn in a college or university is, largely, how to maneuver through a complicated institutional setting. Warren was a terrific maneuverer. He taught only two days a week and only in the fall term, when the leaves were turning and the air was crisp and New Haven was relatively pleasant. In the spring, when it was slushy and cold and foggy and dreadful, he went off to Italy or the south of France. Who would not, if he had his druthers?

We would come in and arrange ourselves and Warren would read, sometimes quite long stories. Kipling's "The Man Who Would Be King" takes a long time to read aloud. And we'd have to pay attention, because Warren's odd Kentucky twang was unfamiliar enough that we'd have to listen hard just to catch some of the words. He had a commanding presence, his face having been deformed into a peculiar cragginess by his loss of an eye (in childhood, his brother had thrown a stone that had hit him) and his having been stung almost to death as a young man by a swarm of bees. Age and prestige had modified these defects into a monumentality that he could use when he wanted to or could play against, flashing a quick, warm smile.

I brought him short stories to look at, and poems, too, on occasion, even though poetry wasn't, strictly speaking, a part of the course. But Warren's range was an important demonstration. In the fifties, it was considered somehow undignified if not quite disgraceful for a poet to write novels. One novel was permissible—Allen Tate had written *The Fathers*—but to go on and have a career as a poet-novelist was eccentric. Robert Graves was doing it in Europe. In America, Warren was almost unique. And even beyond the poetry and novels and short stories, there were the essays, some of them academic, some of them more journalistic. Cleanth Brooks, Warren's collaborator and close friend, once made a wry comparison between the two of them, pointing out that unlike his friend Warren, he was working "without a net." Another way to look at that extraordinarily diverse set of achievements was to observe, as Richard Sewall had done, that Warren was keeping alive the tradition of the man of letters, playing all the games on the literary midway to see how good he was in different genres and, perhaps more important, to discover what each of them might elicit.

The most significant aspect of Warren's presence for me, how-

ever, was that, unlike Dudley Fitts, who was an ex-poet, Warren was
still writing and actively publishing. If he didn't knock himself out
as a teacher, that was not only because he didn't altogether believe in
it, but also because he was saving his energies. He'd come up to New
Haven from Redding Road in Fairfield, Connecticut, an enclave of
gentleman farmers just outside the depression of Bridgeport, and he
would do his thing, one or two days a week, for fourteen weeks a
year. The rest of his time was his own.

Warren spent most of his life as an academic—at Vanderbilt,
LSU, the University of Minnesota, and Yale—but just from reading
his poetry and fiction, no one could guess that or could suppose that
these long periods of employment had meant much to him. He was
there without letting it get to him, which was, whether he intended it
or not, another valuable lesson for those of us who were sprawled on
those Silliman couches. We all wanted to write, and most of us had
toyed with the idea of being writers, which is a slightly different kind
of commitment. But we didn't have very clear ideas about how to do
either of these things. With those kinds of questions in our minds,
we regarded Warren as an enormously important figure. It was reassuring that he took us seriously. Just to see him and hear him talk
about literature in a more writerly rather than professorial way was
fascinating. We learned from his acuteness; we also learned from his
curious negligence—these classes that were almost jokes turned out,
in the long run, to be extraordinarily instructive.

Was this what he intended? I have no idea, and it was hardly the
kind of question I could ever ask him, even later, on those four or
five occasions when we met after I graduated. My hunch, though, is
that he was the way he was, and Yale could take it or leave it. What
he published when I was an undergraduate wasn't the wonderful poetry of his later phase (*Promises: Poems, 1954–1956* appeared after I
graduated) but *Band of Angels,* a novel I thought was terrible, a wal-
low in Southern gothic sex and slavery somewhere between *Gone
with the Wind* and *Mandingo* that, like water, found its proper level in
the 1957 Raoul Walsh movie with Clark Gable, Yvonne DeCarlo,
and Sidney Poitier that came out from Warner Brothers.

With some chagrin, I record the fact that I reviewed *Band of Angels* for the *Yale Daily News,* saying that it was a really bad book, and

then, assuming that Warren would never have seen my review, taking my copy to him for his inscription. Either my assumption or hope was correct and he hadn't read the review, or else he was amused by my nerve and, with the Warner Brothers check having cleared, invulnerable to any undergraduate's disapproval, but he did, indeed, write on the flyleaf, "To David Slavitt, Best Regards, Robert Penn Warren."

It's the only book of his I have with his inscription, and of course, it turned out to be exactly the right one, although in 1955, I couldn't have suspected that I would go on to do *The Exhibitionist* and *The Voyeur* as Henry Sutton. Warren was my model and authority, not only for the combination of poetry and fiction, and literary and journalistic essays, but of high and low, too. (I tried to make it up to him later, when I reviewed *The Cave* in *Newsweek*, praising it probably more than it deserved in my anonymous review. He'd have seen that review but wouldn't have had any way of knowing that I'd written it.)

I have looked at *Band of Angels* recently, and I'm afraid my judgment hasn't changed much, or not about the book anyway. What I know now, and couldn't have imagined then, was that books don't have to be good to be important. This was a novel that Warren almost certainly wrote for the money, and if he didn't then he should have. It was a Literary Guild selection and then a movie, and I expect he made a good deal from it.

I cannot decide how calculated a commercial enterprise it was. My supposition is that it began as a serious enough idea, but developed into the vulgar extravagance that it became, and that Albert Erskine, his friend and editor at Random House, encouraged him. But Warren was not altogether without taste and must have suspected what he had on his desk. From my own experience, I know what it takes to do that kind of book, which is not just a certain craftsmanly competence but an ability to bull through and keep going with what feels like an act of impersonation. It must have been a kind of campy fun for Warren, a southerner, to narrate as a young woman who discovers that she's (a) black and (b) a slave, and in that persona gets sent down to New Orleans to be sold on the auction block to a slave trader named Hamish (that is, Ham-ish!) Bond (as in bondsman). She is a passive, not very interesting young woman who discovers that her father, in order to free her before his death, would first have had to declare her to be a slave. With this mixed heritage, she asks, in the first sentence, "Who am I?" and it is with this not terribly profound question that she lives through the Civil War.

The hard part in writing such a book is to maintain the arrogance or sangfroid or whatever else it takes to keep going. If you stop and consider what you're doing, or if you broaden the focus of your attention from the sentence to the page, or sometimes even to the paragraph, you are likely to begin to worry too much and may fall into an unprofitable silence. But, then, what's the harm? Bad books disappear. There are enough good ones to keep us busy. The money, meanwhile, if prudently invested, goes on forever. While I was working on *The Exhibitionist*, I sometimes thought of Warren and this book, which wasn't just a less than successful novel, but a disaster—and it didn't ruin Warren or, indeed, do him any harm at all.

What's interesting to me now is that Warren's poetry of that middle period shows some of those same tendencies toward hamming it up as one finds in *Band of Angels*. He was a sophisticated intellectual type who wore the expensive tweed sport coats of the English country gentlemen that Yalies affected back then. But in his poetry, he was pretending to the bib overalls and wide-brimmed hats of the country boy—of whom there were very few in Fairfield, Connecticut. Some of that was a way of invoking his youth and his roots. But he really worked it as Tate seldom did, and as Ransom would do only rarely and briefly with an unusual phrase or an oddly omitted article. Warren used his twang (from Kentucky, it was more nasal and faster than a real drawl) as a way to achieve a pastoral distance and thereby manage certain calculated effects. For a subtle, sophisticated poet like him to choose meters that are more appropriate to patter songs and barroom routines could not have been inadvertence.

> In the age of denture and reduced alcoholic intake,
> When the crow's dawn-calling stirs memory you'd better eschew,
> You will try the cross, or the couch, for balm for the heart's
>   ache—
> But that stranger who's staring so strangely, he knows you are you.

Things are getting somewhat out of hand now—light falls on the
    marshes.
In the back lot the soft-faced delinquents are whistling like snipe.
The apples you stored in the cellar are acerb and harsh as
The heart that on bough of the bosom all night will not ripe.

Burn this poem, though it wring its small hands and cry *alack*.
But no use, for in bed, into your pajama pocket,
It will creep, and sleep as snug as a field mouse in haystack,
And its heart to your heart all night make a feather-soft racket.

The foregoing stanzas, the conclusion of "Clearly about You," the
first poem in "Garland for You" in *You, Emperors, and Others* is a
good example of the kinds of devices Warren was discovering at
about the time I was one of his students. It is a successful piece, I
think, but quirky, doing things that nobody else would do, showing
off with its jokiness of the "eschew" and "you" rhyme, or, even
more impishly, "marshes" rhyming with "harsh as" and using "ripe"
as a rustic version of "ripen."

Joseph Blotner reports in his biography of Robert Penn Warren
that Allen Tate once remarked to his friend Walter Sullivan that "Red
had no ear for the spoken language, that he ran his words together
and that the rhythm of his sentences was wrong," but I think Tate
just didn't understand that the exaggerations and distortions were
deliberate and that, when the constellations were right, Warren could
work these apparent deformities into a heightened rhetoric that he
could use to marvelous effect. His remarks, in class and in print,
about other people's poetry demonstrated very clearly that he could,
indeed, read and respond to rhythms and that he had an ear for the
language. (It was Brooks, with whom I also studied, who seems
never to have harkened to the music of a line of verse.)

Warren's poem, after all, is not at all unserious in its intention and
effect. The "crow's dawn-calling" is a typical Warrenesque hyphen-
ation, just a little highfalutin, but those country types will use odd locutions like that, won't they? In those bib overalls, there may well be
a tattered Virgil in one of the pockets. "Alack" is a word I don't think
I've ever heard anyone express aloud in a moment of actual grief or

dismay. It's rural talk, and literary (it is "this poem" that makes the exclamation, after all), and it goes with the apples in the cellar, the whistling of the snipe, and the "field mouse in haystack"—which, without its article, is even more backcountry than it might be otherwise. The strategies are not altogether different from those of Frost but southern, of course, and, as with a number of Frost's poems, the jokes conspire and turn dark at the end.

It is a risky manner of proceeding, as we can see in a less successful venture, "A Real Question Calling for Solution," which is number 5 in that same suite. It begins:

> Don't bother a bit, you are only a dream you are having,
> And if when you wake your symptoms are not relieved,
> That is only because you harbor a morbid craving
> For belief in the old delusion in which you have always believed.
>
> Yes, there was the year when every morning you ran
> A mile before breakfast—yes, and the year you read
> Virgil two hours just after lunch and began
> Your practice of moral assessment, before the toothbrush and bed.
>
> But love boiled down like porridge in a pot,
> And beyond the far snow-fields westward, redder than hate,
> The sun burned; and one night much better forgot,
> Pity, like sputum, gleamed on the station floor-boards, train late.

That last stanza would be tough to get away with, even with a guitar, a cowboy hat, and a rhythm section behind you. But the voice that strikes us here as almost absurd seems on other occasions to have been enabling to the poet. But then, as Warren continued into what is generally called his later phase—the poems from the seventies onward—he needed these eccentricities less and less. Those late poems are more confident, more naked, slightly more conventional in their diction. He tends to bloviate, and he will still clown around some, but the posturing could work for him and it was, in a way, a part of his philosophy of composition as expressed in the early essay he wrote, "On Pure and Impure Poetry," the implications of which he continued to explore for decades.

The point of that essay is that Romeo's loftiness and idealism require Mercutio's dirty jokes outside the garden, and that the two combine to make a representation of life that would be, without both elements together, partial and unconvincing. Warren sees proprieties as limitations and exclusions, and his appetite for inclusiveness, which is what makes him so valuable a poet, can lead him either to a wonderful persuasiveness or, on occasion, into utter catastrophe.

What Paul Weiss told me about studying with great men turns out to have been the best advice anyone ever gave me. Warren's career, erratic and peculiar as it was, has been enabling. I think back to those days almost half a century ago and consider among my classmates which were the ones with talent and promise, and I was in the group but by no means the brightest of the stars. There were others who were more dazzling, who talked a great game, or who even wrote well. But talent is only a small part of what makes a writer. The rest is a matter of luck and determination and character—not nobility so much as bullheadedness. Or maybe just the inability to imagine any other kind of life. I have been encouraged not only by the successes Warren enjoyed but also by the failures he shrugged off. The uneven quality of the novels and even of the poems, and the bizarre relationship he had to academic life, which he clearly enjoyed even while circumventing its absurd requirements, were liberating and reassuring. In the long run—even in the medium run—the failures are unimportant. Success, also, turns out to be unimportant. It's the achievement that counts, whether the world recognizes it or not.

At an award ceremony of the American Academy of Arts and Letters in the late spring of 1989, I saw Eleanor Clark, Warren's wife, and I asked after him. And did it wrong. I was fifty-four years old and "Professor Warren" wasn't appropriate. I knew his friends called him "Red," but that seemed presumptuous. So I asked her to "give Robert my warmest regards," and she corrected me, sharply I thought: "Red. His friends call him Red."

Of course, as I realized a few seconds later, she was including me among his friends, so it wasn't so sharp a correction after all. To retrieve the moment, I did have the wit to ask how he was. And she answered that he was not well at all.

I asked if I might come up to visit. She said yes, but I should call first. And a few months later, I did call and did visit. I came by late one summer morning, driving up from where I'd been visiting in western Massachusetts and crossing into Vermont. "Red"—I can do it, but only with the quotes—had lost a lot of weight and looked terrible but he was cordial and apparently pleased to see me. He invited me to stay to lunch. I looked to Eleanor, who nodded but warned me that I should leave right after the meal so that he could have his nap.

At one point, he went off to the bathroom and Eleanor told me that for my visit Warren had cut back on his pain medication so as to be alert. I was as expeditious as I could be about getting out of there and, indeed, that was all I could think about. I hardly remember what we talked about.

But whatever combination of pride or affection, whether for me individually or just as a representative of all the students he'd had during all those years of teaching, what his gesture clearly meant was that my visit counted for him. What else was there to say?

Poetic Justice

THE DAY I REMEMBER WITH greatest clarity of my four years as a Yale undergraduate was the one on which Stephen Spender and then Robert Frost appeared and I saw that poetry wasn't just a literary genre but, literally, a blood sport.

Spender had come two or three years before to read poems, so this time, when he offered Norman Holmes Pearson the choice of a reading or a lecture, Pearson suggested that, for variety's sake, the lecture might be agreeable. Spender said he would be happy to deliver it.

Happy, though, turned out not to be quite the right word. The trouble was that Cleanth Brooks introduced Spender. Cleanth, a short, courtly southerner with thick eyeglasses and steel-gray hair, initiated the proceedings with a typically graceful few words from the stage of the large lecture hall in S.S.S. (Sterling Sheffield Strathcona Hall) and then sat down on an armchair at the side of the stage. Spender—not yet Sir Stephen, for this was 1955, I think—shambled to the lectern, drew a sheaf of folded pages from his jacket pocket, and commenced to talk, the burden of his message being that we should never trust any critic who was not, himself, a poet. Ostensibly, he was attacking F. R. Leavis, but it was malapropos here, because Cleanth, on the stage with him, motionless, as if he were trying somehow to disappear into the crewel work of the large chair on which he sat, was a critic who was not, himself a poet. (Or, even worse, he'd published a couple of poems as a young man but then decided to give it up.)

It was an uncomfortable forty-five minutes, and, to make it even worse, there was a page missing from Spender's lecture—which mattered perhaps less than he thought, and for which, as I later learned, there was a glorious precedent. Dame Edith Sitwell—Litt. D., Litt. D., Litt. D., her letterhead proclaimed, because she had three of them—had two lecture fees, a thousand dollars and the bargain rate of five hundred, for which she would do every other page of the thousand-dollar lecture, giving a flavor of her style but with some of the intricacy of the argument withheld. This, anyway, was the word I'd heard in the Elizabethan Club.

Spender's missing page, however, had no such assertive elegance. Tall, gangly, and awkward, he was rather like one of those bowler-hatted twits in a Monty Python routine. He was also, I thought then and still think, a dismally bad poet. The one Spender line we all knew was the opening of his best-known poem, "I think continually of those who were truly great." There are two adverbs in it, a sure sign that we are being told what to feel rather than given something that might legitimately arouse our feelings. It is, quite unintentionally, a funny line, because it invites the reader to supply at that point the names of Auden, Louis MacNeice, and Day Lewis, with whom Spender was always associated and of whose greatness he might well have been thinking often if not continually.

He was trendy in ways that seem dated now and nearly quaint. He was anti-Georgian, and showed his modernity with aggressively urban and industrial images, so that he could say, with a perfectly straight face, addressing a beloved that he "turned away, / Thinking, if these were tricklings through a dam, / I must have love enough to run a factory on, / Or give a city power, or drive a train."

I'm not being hideously unfair. I seem not to have a volume of

Spender's poetry on my shelves, and those lines are from the *Oxford Book of Twentieth-Century English Verse* (chosen by Philip Larkin), presumably because the five poems Larkin included were the best that Spender had produced.

Spender's strengths and weaknesses as a poet had little to do with the argument he was making, but it now strikes me that Auden has written somewhere that practicing poets are unreliable critics, preferring what they can learn from, or can steal, to those qualities that an impartial reader might value. Still, even then, in the lecture hall, while I didn't have that counterargument to what Spender was proposing to us, I remember being unconvinced. I was also puzzled about why there needed to be any a priori judgment of any kind about what kind of critic was better than what other kind. Why couldn't we just decide, on a case-by-case basis, whose insights were shrewd, or useful, or entertaining, or provocative? In any event, Dr. Leavis's influence was not high on my list of intellectual problems. And, like everyone else in the room, I was uncomfortable for Cleanth's sake.

That evening, Frost was appearing at Pierson College. He was a fellow of the college and came by every year. He would do a reading, meet with a few of the literary students in the living room of the master's residence, and then spend the night in the Pierson guest quarters. It was an elaborately honed performance. He knew what he was doing, having done it so many times before. Frost, after all, more or less invented the college poetry reading and by then he was making a substantial part of his living from these gigs. The common room was quite full, and *le tout* New Haven was there—Pearson, Brooks, Spender, faculty members from other residential colleges, and of course members of Pierson College.

Frost's guise was the old codger, hard of hearing, except when he wanted not to be, rambling, almost aimlessly, but with a sharpness that this pose made all the more startling. I remember that on two or three visits he read, "Provide, Provide," or, to use the term he preferred, he *said* that poem to us. And the ending was not quite what he had on the page:

Some have relied on what they knew,
Others on being simply true.
What worked for them might work for you.

No memory of having starred
Atones for later disregard,
Or keeps the end from being hard.

Better to go down dignified
With boughten friendship at your side
Than none at all. Provide, provide!

He paused a moment, and then added, mischievously, "Or somebody else will provide for you," and when that got the small, uncomfortable chuckle it was supposed to get, topped that with the next line, "And how would you like that?"

These must have begun as spontaneous remarks, almost inadvertent filler, a part of the patter a poetry reading requires because no audience can supply for very long that kind of heightened attention poetry requires. It would be exhausting. And Frost was a skillful enough performer to know that he had to let us relax a little, recoup, and regather our wits and emotions. But this taunting of conventional liberalism had become a part of the routine, reliable and habitual. The throwaway lines had all but joined the poem itself. They were part of the pose that allows or even demands the "boughten," which is defiantly folksy. The implied claim is that this is hard-won country wisdom. (It may, indeed, have been hard-won, but there was nothing of the rube in Frost.)

He did his maundering, offering his familiar remarks about free verse, and then, more generally, about freedom to and freedom from, which are quite different. And then, as if the thought had just that minute occurred to him but hadn't been prompted by anything so vulgar as an actual occasion, something or someone out there in the external world, he threw in a line that wasn't familiar: "You know, there are a lot of fifth-rate poets who, without their social conscience, might be third rate."

It ran right by me, and by many of my classmates, I have no doubt. But Spender was smart enough to know that he'd been insulted. Perhaps Pearson and Brooks and some of the others had sneaked glances at him, or maybe not sneaked but looked, candidly, to see how he'd behave now that the afternoon's shoe was on the other foot. Nobody smiled. But that was because nobody had to. It was nice, and deft, and done with. Or it could have been, if Spender had been inclined to tough it out. But he was, as I've suggested, very tall, and he felt conspicuous. And he decided that perhaps the best thing for him to do was to withdraw.

It wasn't an altogether catastrophic plan, but he was also clumsy as some tall Brits are. And he hadn't noticed that if he was going to try to leave through the French doors, it was essential to look down and see where the electrical cord went from the outlet to the lamp beside the grand piano. Not having watched exactly where he was putting his feet, he tripped over the wire and fell through the glass doors and onto the flagstones outside, with a shattering of glass and, actually, blood from his cut hands.

A painful business, and we were worried. Heads turned toward the door and the fallen figure out there who lay stretched out on the flagstones. And Frost?

He waited until the first moment of excitement had passed, asked, "What was that?" and then answered his own question: "Nothing important, I'm sure."

What was I to make of all this? It is generally known that Frost could be . . . frosty. I can't remember who it was who told me about some editor inviting him to be part of an anthology of America's hundred greatest poets and his declining with the quip that is probably true: "America hasn't had a hundred great poets." Spender's fall and his bloodied hands weren't Frost's responsibility but the result of the British poet's own clumsiness. Frost's oblique and incidental insult was a kind of twitting that seems perfectly appropriate in the light of Spender's own performance a few hours earlier. Poetic justice, call it. All I can imagine Frost would have reasonably expected would have been Spender having to sit there in discomfort for a couple of minutes, which was less than what Brooks had had to suffer up on the stage.

All that is true enough, but beside the point, I think, which was something quite different and much more important: Frost thought of himself as a better poet than Spender. And therefore, Spender was an annoyance, even an affront.

We spend our lives at this, working hard, demanding of ourselves a standard of excellence that we can only occasionally meet. We have our moments—and months—of doubt and even despair, and we worry that we will never be able to write another poem again. Or that the poems we have written weren't as good as we'd wanted, and we've been kidding ourselves, wasting our time in a delusional and pathetic enterprise. We learn to be tough with ourselves, even brutal. And that brutality is a part of our aspiration, is allied somewhere to the best that is in us.

Sometimes, it comes out and shows itself, as it did that evening. Frost was being brutal to poor Spender, but nowhere near as brutal as he would habitually be to himself.

"I think continually of those who were truly great"?

Trip him. Throw him through that French door and out onto the patio.

No, maybe not. But to ride him a little, to make a remark that might cause him an instant's distress? I can see that.

And the remark afterward, the really cruel one, about "Nothing important, I'm sure," isn't just Frost speaking. It's poetry, itself.

It's a phrase that goes through my head a lot, almost half a century later. Sometimes, I'm Frost. More often, I'm Spender, out there in the night bleeding and hearing the line and the laughter of undergraduates, sharper than any glass shards.

John Hall
Wheelock

I HAD THE PLEASURE RECENTLY of reading a transcription of John Hall Wheelock's contribution to the Columbia University oral history project, which is about to be published and which amounts to an autobiography, albeit informal as taped talk tends to be.[1] Wheelock chose me as the last of his Poets of Today, an adventurous series Scribner's brought out, less, I think, from any commitment to publishing poetry than as a way of thanking Wheelock for his many years of service to the firm—and also because Charles Scribner IV, the proprietor of the firm at the time, had figured out the gimmick of publishing three poets' first books bound together in one volume. Each of the poets would have friends and family, and each would have gone to school somewhere. . . . If you took these "gimme" sales that even a vanity press publication can assume and

1. *The Last Romantic: An Oral Autobiography by John Hall Wheelock*, edited by Matthew J. Bruccoli with Judith S. Baughman; foreword by George Garrett (University of South Carolina Press, 2002).

multiplied them by three, you would come close to breaking even, even before the sales to the general public. You wouldn't make a lot of money with any of these books, but you'd be limiting your losses. The appeal of that kind of merchandising strategy would have been what caught the imagination of the bean counters, who are usually the people editors have to fight to get books of poems published.

The bean counters have won, clearly, and very few trade presses bring out any poetry at all these days. With only a few exceptions, they have abandoned the field to the university presses, which are themselves beleaguered and fighting for survival. Wheelock represents the twilight of a quite different and rather better time—when publishers at least paid lip service to quality, and some houses— Scribner's, with its profitable backlist, was lucky enough to be one of them—could afford to make decisions that were not merely the results of number crunching.

As I read his reminiscences, I saw how much he was a figure of another era. He talks about how, crossing on the ferry to Long Island, his father held him up—he was two or three years old at the time—and called his attention to a bearded figure at the prow of the boat. Wheelock had no recollection of actually seeing Walt Whitman—as he puts it, with his "physical eyes," but he did remember being told that he'd seen the great man. Elsewhere, he talks about sailing to England one summer to lurk outside Swinburne's house in Putney in London for three days, just to get a glimpse of that poet he so much admired.

He was born on September 9, 1886, and he went to Harvard, from which he graduated in 1908, when George Santayana, William James, George Lyman Kittredge, Charles Townsend Copeland, and Irving Babbitt were all teaching there, and where he was a couple of classes behind T. S. Eliot and Conrad Aiken. Wheelock's early and middle poetry is more or less comparable to that of the British Georgians, but then, quite late in life, after his retirement from Scribner's, when he took up his pen again, he found a surer mode of expression, a refinement of and improvement upon what had gone before. His work, in that way, is like that of Yeats. As Henry Taylor observes in *Compulsory Figures* in the best essay I know about Wheelock's poetry, "It is worth remarking, in a spirit of gratitude, that a poet could survive so many years and so many mediocre poems, and come to write, in his seventies and eighties, work that constitutes one of the notable achievements in our literature."

I am not only a reader but a partisan of these poems—as a poet's readers ought, perhaps, to be. Many of these poems are about old age and about the house out on Long Island where he grew up and where he moved through the gardens his father had planted and tended, in a settled kind of existence that few Americans can imagine, let alone enjoy. It was to that house that I came in 1959, early on in my career at *Newsweek,* to interview him about his series and his career as a publisher and poet. *Poets of Today VI* was about to be published, with the work of Gene Baro, Donald Finkel, and Walter Stone. (The spine, therefore, announces, Baro Finkel Stone: and there is a novel, I believe by Leslie Fiedler, in which Baro Finkelstone appears as a minor character.)

My motive in going out there was simply to interview Wheelock and do what I thought might be an interesting piece of reportage. It still seems like a quirky enough and therefore tempting enough situation. . . . Those three-in-one volumes were, on the one hand, a little gimmicky, but then, on the other, they were a very impressive series, with the debuts of a number of successful poets, and, just as interesting, a number of fine performances by poets who have not gone on to do anything else. Walter Stone, for instance, was dead when *Poets of Today VI* was published, and to bring his work to the attention of the public crossed the line from bravery into recklessness.

But the list of poets to whom Wheelock gave their start is impressive. May Swenson, Robert Pack, Louis Simpson, Joseph Langland, George Garrett, Robert Wallace, O. B. Hardison Jr., Donald Finkel, and James Dickey were all "Poets of Today." For a series that lasted only eight years, that is an amazing roster, launching a higher proportion of interesting and valuable careers than the Yale Younger Poets series, for which W. H. Auden, Dudley Fitts, and, more recently, W. S. Merwin have served as arbiters. Wheelock, of course, was an experienced and shrewd editor, who worked with—and did much of the work for—the more famous Maxwell Perkins. It was Wheelock who first read and championed James Jones's *From Here to*

Eternity. He made mistakes from time to time, as the reminiscences admit—most particularly with *Under the Volcano,* which he "passed" on and shouldn't have. But as an editor—which is to say a chooser—of poetry, he had an uncanny accuracy. If some of those two dozen did not go on to establish themselves on the American poetry scene, that can happen. Sometimes, it was the choice of the poets. Murray Noss, who was in the first volume, has become an almost legendary figure and was said to have been seen in the sixties and seventies in a chauffeured limousine, roaming around the South, staying at old drummers' hotels, sitting in rocking chairs on their verandas, writing poetry on a Magic Slate, and, reportedly, when he had a poem the way he liked it, lifting the cellophane and letting the poem go. Publication? He'd been there and done that.

In my zanier moods, I can relate to what I think may have been prompting him, for a book publication is a kind of credential. I remember my puzzlement and chagrin after I got out of college and found that it was difficult to get into the quarterlies where I'd appeared with undergraduate work—in the *Yale Review,* the *Kenyon Review,* the *Chicago Review,* and one or two others. But then? Those doors all seemed to have slammed shut. But after the Scribner's imprimatur, it was easier again. I report this very clear recollection not so much to impugn the poetry editors of the literary magazines as to demonstrate the kind of independent judgment that Wheelock was exercising, and to convey something of the scale of my indebtedness to him.

But beyond that certification, there was the publication itself. There hasn't been anything like that experience, not with any of the eighty books that have followed, and I can remember thinking what I expect every one of the "Poets of Today" must have thought, opening up the package and looking for the first time at the advance copies of his book—that whatever else might happen, this was an achievement that would endure. There would be, at the very least, copies of these poems in the major libraries where they were available to readers but, even without readers, might remain on the shelves in a kind of spore state, to be discovered later on in another, perhaps more receptive time.

I don't think the possibility of the publication of my poems in Wheelock's series was anywhere in my mind, though, when I proposed the story at the weekly editorial conference. At twenty-four, I wasn't shrewd enough to think that way. All I wanted, as far as I can remember, was to sneak into the pages of the magazine a piece about poetry, which I enjoyed reading. And if I could do that under the guise of a trade piece on the three-in-one stratagem, that wouldn't compromise my coverage or limit in any way what I could say about Wheelock or the poets he was publishing. *Newsweek*'s ecology, at the time, was particularly hostile to highbrow pretentiousness. John Denson was the editor of the magazine, and he conceived his role as that of a realist who didn't want his writers putting on airs that would alienate readers. The magazine was written for the most part by a group of people who could have passed for faculty members at any respectable liberal arts college and a fair number of us wouldn't even have read the magazine if we hadn't been working for it. To be good enough to do the work, you had to be too good to want to do it.

One can see those stresses in the piece I wrote for the magazine. It wasn't a terrible story, and the remarkable thing was that I got it into the magazine, but it has the glib *Newsweek* tone I'd learned to mimic.

DANCING TO SAD MUSIC

One of the most durable and quietly influential editor-poets in the country is John Hall Wheelock, whose name has long been familiar to almost all American poets but whom hardly anybody else knows at all. With the publication this week of "Poets of Today VI" (Scribner's, $3.95),[2] poet Wheelock, who has edited the annual series since he originated it six years ago, can carve another notch in his already well nicked editorial pencil.

Can I have actually typed such a sentence? Or, to be realistic, can I now decide which would have been worse—for me to have written it or for it to have been inserted by some editor (copy went from me to

2. Poets: Gene Baro, a teacher at Bennington; Donald Finkel, a teacher at Bard; and the late Walter Stone, who taught at Vassar.

the general editor, the senior editor, the managing editor, and then, sometimes, John Denson himself)? Either way, I wince at its smug, unearned knowingness, the vulgar, lapel-grabbing chumminess of the gesture. But that is the worst line of the piece. It continues:

> Two years ago Wheelock, now 73, retired as senior editor at Scribner's, where he had been for 46 years, but he has continued his work on this project, selecting each year three new poets whose work he feels deserves a book, and writing an introduction for each volume.
>
> "I've enjoyed the work," he said last week, on the porch of his 70-year-old home in Easthampton, N.Y., "and I've enjoyed the feeling that I'm helping young poets. Not that I'm a saint; I'm paid—and well paid—for my work by Scribner's, but if I didn't have this series to work on I'd have more time for my own writing."

One was always safer with quotations, which the editors didn't mess with.

> Wheelock is one of those beautiful old men—like Carl Sandburg and Robert Frost—who have, beneath a shock of white hair, the glittering eye and the enthusiasm of a teen-ager; and each quality complements the other. At Scribner's, as successor to the famous Maxwell Perkins, Wheelock wrote very little poetry for much of his time there. He came out with "Collected Poems, 1936" but editorial work was "so absorbing, and so oppressive, that writing was just impossible. But I enjoyed it . . . and that was the trouble. I felt great pride in helping to produce the kind of list that Scribner's always had . . . after all Eliot takes pride in his editing work. Hardy was a reader for Macmillan. Meredith was a reader for Constable. A poet is almost forced to go into teaching or into editorial work of some kind. But it's seductive, and it's not good for him." It was in the late 1940s that Wheelock began writing again, and in 1956 he published "Poems Old and New," in which the new work was surer and even better than anything he had done before. "I hope that by 1961," Wheelock said, "I'll have another book."

Changing the subject to the modern scene in poetry, Wheelock commented: "What I miss in most of the new poets is a feeling of some underlying philosophy. They are too much concerned merely with the presentation of the data of the sense. But the nature of things—it's obvious that it's tragic. And yet, there's a joy in it. There's a line I used once, that I translated from Rilke: 'Move with a dancing step to a sad music.' Of course, the idea is old, and ancient, but it comes close to the truth."

When he was a year old Wheelock saw Walt Whitman once, on a ferryboat in New York Harbor ("My father lifted me above his head, and pointed him out"), and, in his teens, Swinburne passed by him in London, and the young Wheelock reached out and touched his coat. But it was his mother, who loved poetry and who used to read it and recite it to him, that first kindled his love for it. Fortunately, it has been a requited love. "I think there will be a return to poetry, soon," Wheelock said. "It will be getting more attention. With the changes that have come about since Swinburne's time, poetry is able now to deal with the prosaic aspects of life, without being stuffy or pompous any more."

Author-ity: This had a certain authority, coming as it did from a man who at Scribner's voted to take on Fitzgerald's "This Side of Paradise," and who brought in Erskine Caldwell's early book "American Earth," and who has edited Nancy Hale and Santayana, Alan Paton and Allan Nevins, and who was one of the readers for "Look Homeward, Angel," and who remembers Edith Wharton as "very attractive, but stiff. She always reminded me of a wasp."

I reproduce the "author-ity" slug with a twinge. They don't use those anymore, although there are still jazzy gestures in the layout of the magazine to indulge the reader and prevent fatigue. The slug was a way of breaking up a column of text that might otherwise present too imposing an obstacle, with all those words, one after another! Here, let us congratulate you with a little joke, a reward for having got this far, a kind of intellectual Dog-Yummy to keep you alert and reassure you that we care. They also ran, at the end of critical pieces, a "summing-up," which was, ideally, a snappy remark, a way of re-

minding the reader with a short attention span what the general tendency of the review had been; a thumbs-up or -down for the book,
movie, or play under review. I left *Newsweek* in 1965, and it was only
a few years ago, in the midnineties, when I stopped having a recur-
ring nightmare about being back at the magazine and assigned to the
job of permanent summing-up editor, reducing all experience in
some perky way to one and a half lines of thirty-nine characters.

I mention this, not to invite sympathy for myself, but as a way of
poking through Mr. Wheelock's good manners to the truth of his job
at Scribner's, the truth of most jobs in fact, which is that there are
disagreeable things one has to do, and that the trick is to do them
without worrying too much about them. As Ted Robinson, one of
the general editors at *Newsweek,* once said to me, "It isn't important
that the magazine comes out every week. What's important is that I
come out every week." What gives the remark particular force for
me is that eventually Robinson jumped out of a window and killed
himself.

But back to the *Newsweek* piece:

> It is the voice of experience that says, in the introduction to "Poets
> of Today VI," that "A great poem . . . unites men as does any
> great work of art . . . in its presence, the participants and oppo-
> nents . . . come together no longer as such but as disinterested
> spectators of the whole . . . predicament of life."
>
> Next year's "Poets of Today VII" have already been selected,
> and the introduction is done. Wheelock expects to begin looking
> around for contributors to volume VIII when he returns to New
> York in the fall. "All I want," he said pouring a glass of burgundy,
> "is another twelve or fifteen years to work in."

What he got was almost nineteen, and the work kept getting better. He was lean and appeared therefore to be slightly frail, and with
that shock of white hair, he looked very old to the youngster I was.
In the *Newsweek* picture that appears on the page with my piece, he
still looks old, although I'm only six years younger now than he was
then. I remember very little of our conversation, but I do still have
an impression of walking through the elaborate gardens behind and

to the side of the house. And I remember that what he communicated wasn't so much the pride of possession but his delight in showing me such a fine thing, as if he weren't the owner but a docent in a museum.

I do remember that at some point he asked me whether I wasn't a poet, too, which I then thought almost uncanny of him, although I realize now that it was an obvious enough question. Why else would the kid have proposed such a story that, surely, could not have been some editor's idea? What else could have prompted the young reporter's interest? And, anyway, many of the writers at *Time* and *Newsweek* had been undergraduate poets or short-story writers who had settled or temporized and hired themselves out. The job was, and still may be, every English major's dream. I told him that, yes, I wrote poetry, and had even published here and there. He invited me to send him some. And I wound up in that *Poets of Today VIII* I'd written about. It was the last volume of the series.

The *Newsweek* piece was not the only thing I wrote about my trip out to Easthampton. There was also a poem that came out of the experience, one I put into the manuscript and that Wheelock liked but for obvious reasons didn't want to include in the book he was publishing. It appeared in *The Carnivore,* my second book, that came out in 1965.

ELEGY FOR WALTER STONE

In August of 1959, I interviewed John Hall Wheelock at his home in Easthampton, N.Y., on the occasion of the publication of Poets of Today VI, *which Mr. Wheelock edited and which included the poetry of Messrs. Gene Baro, Donald Finkel, and Walter Stone.*

I

In the Apache over Hempstead with Finkel's view
of Fuji and the great wave in my hand . . .
But who would pretend to care? And why should Finkel
(not this particular Finkel, but any Finkel)

have a view of Fuji?
                                    So I wondered whether
there was a first-rate delicatessen in all Japan.
An odd business this—when the mind takes off
leaving the body's ground, and the old terrain
with height is suddenly strange and unfamiliar,
when woods are smoothed to shrubbery, to lawn,
to plain green as the U.S. on a map,
when a Fuji is smoothed to paint, and paint to print,
and a craggy Finkel to an anonymous voice.
And the last is worst.
                                    In London, on a grant
to study Renaissance eschatology,
the late professor and poet, Walter Stone,
committed suicide: an actual man
ground to a sheaf of poems that follow Finkel's
and in their total commitment to aesthetics
go his one better, for somewhere, still, in hiding,
in Queens, or perhaps the Bronx, surreptitious, Finkel
munches pastrami on rye (and afterwards
his tongue hunts for the caraway seeds in the teeth),
giving less of a damn for Fuji than, even, I.
Vive le Finkel! Which is exactly the point.

But let me be honest, for I too am a poet,
and the poet, Stone, is survived by a poet, his wife,
Ruth. And by Finkel (not my conceit, but the real
Donald Finkel, who lives and teaches at Bard),
and by his former students,
                                    and by three daughters
who ought to despise that rising, the lyric thrust
that can take a man up where he only guesses at Hempstead,
sees something important in a dead Japanese volcano,
writes—as Stone did—stanzas about a spider
so fine he forgets about his daughters and wife,
forgets even himself, and the piece of work
that a man is, speechless and on the earth.

II

Later: at night: remembering the plane
and the quick trip out to visit John Hall Wheelock.
We savored the horror of it on the porch
and then went in to lunch.

                                        Hart Crane

I can understand. Jumping overboard
was, for him, the perfectly fitting gesture,
with all the grief of his failings as a man,
and still a passing insult to his readers
who cared for the wrong and expendable things.

                                        But Stone

envied the angels' monotonous excellence,
their tuning-fork perfection, their effortlessness,
and even perhaps their wings . . .

                        The weights of the world

he shrugged off him, as if in a moment of pique:
his shoes, for example, in rows on some closet floor;
and his family, and his automobile, and his hairbrush;
and Vassar College itself where the grass grows green
and the laundry washes two thousand bras a week.
The stupid stuff of the world . . .

                        He renounced it all,

or perhaps it was a kind of an embrace,
to become, after an unpleasant moment of choking
(or do you feel even that? Does the neck snap
like a pretzel stick and the life go out in an instant
without that terrible dwindling?), like a stone,
like a table, a part of that same dumb stuff
(with a frozen smile for the possible play on his name).
Not merely the notion of rest, but to be a part
of the created world, to rot, to change,
to become absolutely chemical, and Godly:
this, perhaps, is more the poet's delusion,
fitting the paradoxical turn of the mind
which rejects itself by its own final thought.

Suddenly, there he was, as dead as a door,
and full of the same dignity as the door
in its wonderful knowledge of the real nature of substance.

Or did he wander off in that dark wood
to visit the *malebolges,* where they talk
in terza rima, suddenly convinced . . .
But no!
      Next I'll be calling out the dolphins
and making him into a hapless youth.

                         He died

taking his motive with him, and leaving us
to guess what his question was that had no answer,
and to think, with awe, of a man dead in his prime.

   III

The plane banked to the left and suddenly landed
as gracefully as a sea bird on a rock,
and I stepped out into the forenoon sun
and the salt smell of the wind coming off the ocean,
and felt that slight irrational sense of relief
that the plane had made it all right, and I was standing
there, on the ground, waving to Mr. Wheelock
who had a cab there, waiting. He told me how
he had once refused to go up in a plane with Lindbergh,
and smiled and remarked on the weather as we rode.
Nineteenth century outside and eighteenth in,
his house stands on a rise with a grove of trees
around it. Seventy summers it has been
standing there, where no other house is in view,
and seventy summers John Hall Wheelock has lived
through the rooms of his father's house, and over the lawns.
But it is not virtue:
                    some of the good die young,
and some live long, and life is a random thing,
and the bus careens indifferently up on the sidewalk,
and the lightning, witless, streaks down into the park,

and the virus floats on the universal air.
It is not virtue, but a lucky chance
to which we attach perhaps too much importance
(and how we despise any quitting while you're ahead).
Wheelock was calm about it—regretful, but calm—
as we talked of Walter Stone, and then moved on
to talk of poetry or old pewter,
but there is no changing of subject at seventy-three,
and all the time he talked in one gentle tone
of the various guises of the one same thing
that a man must learn to gaze at, more and more:
Stone dead, and the poems left behind,
and the poems he would leave himself, and the pewter
and the house his father left, and the afternoon
perceptibly giving way.
                                        Never mind how,
and never mind even when. All death is nature's,
whether by germ in the blood or idea in the head,
or sudden mischance in the wasteful order of things.
Gaze fixedly at it, and the distinctions
disappear.
                    An unintellectual sadness
and a dumb calm is all I can summon up
for Walter Stone, for Wheelock, for myself,
for the act of imagination in Finkel's Fuji—
for all these sparks struck off by the turning world.

There are patches I'd do differently now, or omit entirely. But I think it holds up well enough, and there are passages to which I have reverted from time to time during the four decades that have elapsed, so that they are now beyond criticism but just there, a part of my mental landscape. The ending, I think, is recognizably my voice. I am relieved to be able to report that Donald Finkel, whom I met some years later, took the poem in good grace and we have become friends.

What had impressed me and moved me to take up my pen was the connection Wheelock talked about with the landscape and the house, the intensity of that rootedness. It was something he wrote about himself. One of his best poems—he produced it some years after our interview—is "The Gardener," about his father. He omits some of that parent's wackiness that he talked about in the oral history tapes. His father went to the College of Physicians and Surgeons in New York City, but then, after graduation, realized that he didn't like blood and was so neurotic about sickness that whenever a member of his family was unwell, he would take to his bed himself. He then went to law school, graduated from that, and passed the bar, but he found the law disputatious and disliked the confinement of work in an office. So he studied botany and got a job at New York's Botanical Gardens, up in the Bronx. That didn't work out either, and he spent most of the rest of his life playing the French horn and gardening. This is a character who could have appeared in Chekhov, or, with just a little exaggeration, in a Kaufman and Hart play. But he was a decent man, a good father, and Wheelock loved him, which is clear from the poem:

THE GARDENER
(In memory of any father)

Father, whom I knew well for forty years
Yet never knew, I have come to know you now—
In age, make good at last those old arrears.

Though time, that snows the hair and lines the brow,
Has equalled us, it was not time alone
That brought me to the knowledge I here avow.

Some profound divination of your own,
In all the natural effects you sought
Planted a secret that is now made known.

These woodland ways, with your heart's labor bought,
Trees that you nurtured, gardens that you planned,
Surround me here, mute symbols of your thought.

Your meaning beckons me on every hand,
Grave aisles and vistas, in their silence, speak
A language that I now can understand.

In all you did, as in yourself, unique—
Servant of beauty, whom I seek to know,
Discovering here the clue to what I seek.

When down the nave of your great elms I go
That soar their Gothic arches where the sky,
Nevertheless, with all its stars will show,

Or when the moon of summer, riding high,
Spills through the leaves her light from far away,
I feel we share the secret, you and I.

All these you loved and left. We may not stay
Long with the joy our hearts are set upon:
This is a thing that here you tried to say.

The night has fallen; the day's work is done;
Your groves, your lawns, the passion of this place,
Cry out your love of them—but you are gone.

O father, whom I may no more embrace
In childish fervor, but, standing far apart,
Look on your spirit rather than your face,

Time now has touched me also, and my heart
Has learned a sadness that yours earlier knew,
Who labored here, though with the greater art.

The truth is on me now that was with you:
How life is sweet, even its very pain,
The years how fleeting and the days how few.

Truly, your labors have not been in vain;
These woods, these walks, these gardens—everywhere
I look, the glories of your love remain.

Therefore, for you now beyond praise or prayer,
Before the night falls that shall make us one,
In which neither of us will know or care,

This kiss, father, from him who was your son.

The grace with which he manages the terza rima is impressive, and
while the statement seems perfectly straightforward, we can see the
rhetorical balance of the sentences, the poise of the contradictions
and resolutions. In there is, for instance, a nice paradox in the divination, which we expect to be supernatural but arises from the "natural effects" the father sought, and that intricacy is quite probably
related to the "secret," which has not merely metaphorically but
quite literally been "planted," and which has been "made known,"
first to the poet and then, through the poem, to the reader.

What I find impressive is that in the antepenultimate stanza, he
says, with a comparable equipoise, substantially what he said to me
in our interview when he cited Rilke's nice line about the contrariety
of a dancing step to sad music. The only gloss that one feels might
be at all helpful would be to mention the line about looking "on your
spirit rather than your face," which connects in a particular way to
Wheelock's personal mythology as expressed in other late poems.
The first of a series of eight sonnets is called "A Garden and a Face,"
although this time the face is female and that of Wheelock's wife:

The countryside that I love best is here,
And in this countryside a certain place,
And in this place a garden, and a face
That in the garden sometimes will appear—
It is the gay face of the gardener, dear
Beyond all others; she it is will brace
The drooping vine-branch, grant the weeds no grace,
In the full green and glory of the year.

Great trees encircle her; her praise shall be
The thrush's song; the sea-wind for delight
Buffets her cheek while, massive in its might,
Around these island solitudes the sea,

Chanting, like voices from eternity,
Will shake the shore with thunders, day and night.

There is a prose poem, which is a most unusual thing in Wheelock's work, called "The Face," and in its odd account of a dream, it makes perfectly clear what these faces mean to the poet. He says:

He was aware, in his dreams, of a face bending over his—a face, neither man's nor woman's, of such transcendent beauty, force, laughing tenderness, and delight, as marked it not of this earth. A pang, some premonition of death itself, struck through him, and he struggled, but his struggles served only to increase the sense of gradual absorption into another being and of the dissolution of his own. The very core of his selfhood seemed about to be dissolved away, and he started up in a frenzy, when that face of inexorable compassion transfixed him with a smile, a glance, so divine, that in an instant all was comprehended. He yielded, his heart over flowed, pouring on to meet this exultant love. And, in that instant, as he surrendered what so desperately, since the hour of birth, he had fought to preserve, it became clear to him that this was the goal toward which, without knowing it, he had, his whole life long, been laboring with every breath he drew. Time fell away. All consciousness of self was lost. There remained only the face and his adoration of it. Then this, too, passed. He had become a part of what he loved.

Adrien
Stoutenburg

I WAS STILL AT *NEWSWEEK* when I reviewed Adrien Stoutenburg's first book of poems, *Heroes, Advise Us,* for the *New York Herald Tribune*'s *Book Week.* It was just a matter of dumb luck that
Richard Kluger, the editor, should have picked me to do this book. I
had never heard of her, which is not surprising, and what I must have
done then was what I'd do now, which is to check the spine (Scribner's was then a good house and had published my first book a couple of years earlier) and the acknowledgments (the *New Yorker,
Commonweal, The Nation,* the *Yale Review, Saturday Review, Shenan-
doah*). My guess was that somebody at the *Trib* must have done that,
too, dipped into it, and then must have liked it a lot. There are always
too many books competing for too little space, and for the editors to
have decided to send this out for review meant that it must have
knocked somebody's socks off.

I liked it too, and wrote a review that said what I still think is true:
that it was a tough, unflinching collection of extraordinarily skillful
poems. Stoutenburg's most striking characteristic was her ability to

stare at catastrophe without exaggerating or sentimentalizing and wring truth from the encounter. The long poem that gives the collection its title is about the ill-fated expedition of Robert F. Scott and his four companions who, as Stoutenburg reminds us in her epigraph, "reached the South Pole in January, 1912, only to find that they had been preceded by Roald Amundsen. All five perished on the return journey." It is not a cheerful story, but she was able to take a stoic comfort in the determination of these men. The ending of the thirty-nine-page poem still strikes me as quite wonderful in its understated eloquence:

> The epoch lingers and the dead stay dead,
> though nothing in these latitudes can perish.
> Decay is unknown, whether of flesh or language.
> Hands that clasped once are forever clasped,
> and love preserved is forever risen,
> while unchanging eyes, strict as jewels,
> stare through a rent in the woven sky
> at a sky beyond, centered on visions
> we cannot cancel nor revise.

> > *After all, one can go on striving.*
> > *In a brief spell of hope last night*
> > *one heard laughter.*

I remember too—how can one forget it?—"Mirages" and its mention of the horse in the desert and

> . . . How when I kindled an evening fire
> he mistook the flames for water,
> plunged his mouth in and gulped the red fountain,
> screamed like a wire, and leaped upward,
> his nostrils streaming gray roses of smoke . . .
> > > how I went, blinded, back
> to the hair-cloth tents, the herdsmen and housewives,
> the sound of the coffee pestle, the snores of old men,
> the wells stained yellow from pollutions,

my beggar's bowl always extended.
... How I, like Bellerophon before me,
grope through the stalls of dust,
unmoved by hope or hoof or caravan
beneath the nickering sky.

I wrote the review, calling Stoutenburg "the toughest, most unrelenting, most terrifying poet I can think of," sent it off, and was pleased to see it published. I was working for *Newsweek,* reviewing movies, but if my father's habit was to brag sometimes about his son, he would seldom say exactly what I did, mentioning only that I was an "associate editor," but leaving his friends to suppose I was covering national news or doing something serious. That I got up in the morning and went into the city to see an Annette Funicello movie was slightly disgraceful, he thought, and there was a part of me that agreed with him. So for me to be publishing collections of poems and, in a public forum such as the *Trib*'s pages, to be reviewing serious books was a way of redeeming myself.

Actually, I'd been offered the choice at *Newsweek*—books or movies. And I'd picked movies, correctly I still think, because there one could assume that many of the readers might actually go to see the films. In the book section, there could be no such cheerful expectation. The circulation of the magazine was something like three and a half million, which means six or seven million readers, and very few books reach an audience of anywhere near that size. So, a *Newsweek* book reviewer was offering a substitute for the experience of reading the book, while the movie reviewer was spared that inherent awkwardness. But while I understood this and was happier as the flicker-picker, I could see how a lot of people might not get it. Popular culture had not yet become a subject for academic discussion in the sixties, and I therefore enjoyed the respectability of reviewing poetry for the *Trib*.

I was surprised a few weeks later to get a note from Ms. Stoutenburg, forwarded on from the offices of the paper. She said, in part:

> I have to tell you how delighted I was by your review of my HE-ROES, ADVISE US in *Book Week*. If people don't go out and buy

the book, to find out how "terrifying" I am it won't be your fault. In spite of my pleasure, I did think, "My poems aren't really like that." Then I looked over my volume again and decided, "Horrors, the man is right!" It was an original and perceptive review.

I answered her, and she answered me, and we became friends, or, anyway, pen pals, corresponding often over the next seventeen years—until her death in 1982. We met only a couple of times, once at the house in which she and Laura Nelson Baker lived in Lagunitas, in Marin County, across the bridge from San Francisco, and once out in some Boston suburb, where she was visiting a relative. But we exchanged letters, mostly about writing and publishing, but sometimes with personal information. My letters to her are mostly in the Bancroft Library at Berkeley; her letters to me are mostly at the Beinecke at Yale—except for that first letter that I'd tucked into *Heroes, Advise Us* and that surprised me, turning up this morning when I went to find those lines to quote.

She was almost twenty years older than I, and she'd worked as a librarian in Minnesota and had supported herself writing children's books. In many ways, she was like Amy Clampitt, although rather less fussy, technically. But that startling combination of a midwestern directness with an exquisitely refined sensibility came through in the poems and in the letters, too. In theory, one would expect that this kind of thing would happen more often. If literature is, among other things, a conversation, then two poets like her and me, finding affinities of interests and tastes, ought to get on. In actuality, this happens rather rarely, and too often writers can turn out to be competitive, passive-aggressive, manipulative, depressive, or otherwise afflicted with personality defects that they may be able to filter out of what they write but that are troublesome or even intolerable when you encounter them in person.

It is not my purpose here to try to describe that friendship. The letters are on deposit, after all, as we knew they'd be. On my side, anyway, and I think on hers, too, one of the pleasures of the correspondence was that it was so old-fashioned, so literary. We wrote for each other, but were not altogether unmindful of those scholars and even general readers who might, in the middle-distant future, be looking over what we were putting down on the page—not perhaps because we were, ourselves, so interesting or important, but to get an idea of what the literary life felt like in the latter half of the twentieth century.

I have other writer friends, and I am in touch with a number of them, but mostly by e-mail these days. And I am less scrupulous than I should be about printing out every joke or casual exchange of gossip. If one of my colleagues sends me a draft of a poem, or an essay, or a story, I'm likely to print that out and save it (and put it in the Beinecke pile to take down to New Haven next time I drive down there). But I don't keep every scrap, and it may be that the element of posturing with which we began—or with which I began, because, after all, I was much younger—was a good thing. A little self-consciousness can be a prompting toward good manners and stylishness.

However it happened, we became quite good friends, and Adrien actually dedicated her third book, *Greenwich Mean Time,* to me, partly out of friendliness but partly, as I remember, to acknowledge that I'd been helpful as she'd tried to get the collection published. Not that I'd done a whole lot, really. I'd been supportive and encouraging as she'd gone through a number of publishers, getting considered and then rejected. And I told her that it wasn't personal, and that surely it had nothing to do with the poems, which were very good, even better, in some ways, than the pieces in *Heroes, Advise Us.*

Heroes won the Lamont Poetry Award, which was then given to first books. Her second book, *A Short History of the Fur Trade,* came out in 1969, from Houghton Mifflin, and Joyce Carol Oates called it "brilliant," but, as I now see, there were two things that were happening in the po' biz that were adversely affecting Adrien's chances. One was that most trade publishers were abandoning the enterprise entirely, leaving the activity to the university presses. The other was that feminism had hit, and certain female poets had figured out that there were more readers for politics and protest than there were for poetry. If the likes of Adrienne Rich, Marge Piercy, and Denise Levertov were in fashion, then Adrien Stoutenburg wasn't, and the publishing houses are always sensitive to that kind of trend. They don't know about literature, and they don't know about business, but they do know about lunch, and they are good at picking up what's out there in the air, which is a vulgar knack, but then publishing is, in the root sense of the word, vulgar.

Julia Randall, an enormously talented poet whom I know slightly, was dumped by Knopf some years ago, and Alice Quinn, who was the editor there at the time, told her that they were looking for someone who was "younger and more promotable," which would have been offensive in any event but was all the harder to bear when Quinn's new find turned out to be Amy Clampitt, who was several years older than Julia.

But promotable. Which is unfair, but how it is in the world.

It was Gresham's law, with bad poetry driving out good, and I tried to persuade Adrien that she had nothing to worry about, or, at any rate, nothing to blame herself for. Her writing was just fine. And rejections are part of the game. I think the greatest number of rejections any book of mine ever got was somewhere up in the lower thirties, and even though it isn't pleasant, one learns to live with it and to dismiss it. I've been lucky with my poetry, to which Leslie Phillabaum has been astonishingly loyal, first at the University of North Carolina Press and then at LSU. But Phillabaum's plate was full at the time, and Adrien kept getting rejected by the other university presses. I told her what I thought was happening—if you're not a member of one club or another, it's mostly a crapshoot, and not always an honest one, either. There's often an outside reader, who may have his or her own agenda. There can be an exquisite series of near misses, which is what happened to Adrien. I suggested at one point, after she'd been trying for a year or two, that she send the manuscript to the University of Utah Press, where my friend Henry Taylor had just published a book, and which did handsome volumes.

She got lucky there, and they took the book. Henry, indeed, may even have had something to do with it, having perhaps said something about his enthusiasm for her work to Norma Mikkelsen, who was then director of the press. He was on the faculty of the University of Utah at the time. But Adrien was disproportionately grateful to me for what she took to be some kind of miraculous intervention. She thought that I'd fixed it and refused to believe me when I said I'd done almost nothing beyond making that initial suggestion. Hence, the dedication, which, even if it had been prompted by a misunderstanding, was nonetheless delightful.

Years pass, but not so many, and then in 1981 Adrien writes me to say that she has esophageal cancer, and my wife, an oncologist, tells me that the prospects are not good. There is a series of disasters and defeats and, while we do not discuss any of these details in our letters, I find myself wondering whether the unflinching vision of the poetry carries over to the life and is of any help at all. I hope so, but I'm not confident. The voice that speaks in our poetry is often a version of ourselves, but smarter, better, braver.

And then I get a letter of pure joy, in which she reports that, out of the blue, she got a note from James Dickey that said how, in 1965, along with Phyllis McGinley and W. H. Auden, he had been a member of the committee that gave out the Pulitzer Prize for poetry. Ms. McGinley had sprained—or maybe even broken—her ankle and could not participate, so the decision had been left to Auden and Dickey. Auden wanted to give the prize to Richard Howard, while Dickey wanted to give it to Adrien for *Heroes*. There had been much discussion but Auden had prevailed—he was Auden, after all. And Dickey was now writing to say that in the years that have passed, he has gone back to look at Richard Howard's work only rarely and hasn't liked it much, but that he has looked into her book many times, always with pleasure and admiration. And he was writing to say that he was even more convinced now that the decision they'd reached was the wrong one and that she should have had the prize.

They hadn't been in touch at all, didn't even know each other. There had been no way that Dickey could have known that she was dying. But here it was, this amazing letter, letting her at least imagine a whole different career in which she might have enjoyed a discreet, low-level celebrity and in which publishers would have been not only receptive but eager. There could have been offers not only of teaching jobs but of lucrative readings and trips to cultural conferences in exotic places. . . .

It is difficult to look around and see the acrobats and clowns of that circus without envying them just a little. Even as we realize how trivial these things may be, their absence is not correspondingly trivial. We wonder whether we haven't after all been deluding ourselves about the quality of the work that seems largely to have been ignored. The books are there on the shelf, but for the poet to read his own work is a risky enterprise. For one thing, the likelihood of disappointment is greater than that of delighted surprise. We look at these things with a craftsmanly eye and the defects are what strike us. The miracle of the reaction of a stranger's response is precluded, because we aren't the stranger. The spark that leaps from poet—or poem—to reader is what we experience when we remark, in delight or awe, "I've felt just that way, too," but the "too" is very theoretical when we reread our own poetry.

The consequences of this are particularly invidious. We are poets without the poetry and, deprived of all the work we have done in the past, are reduced to a kind of posturing justified, if at all, by plans or hopes about what we may produce in the future. But now Adrien was cut off from the future, too. What Dickey's kind letter suggested was a parallel universe, an alternative to this one, in which there wasn't the dreary decline from an auspicious beginning with the Lamont Prize and good reviews to these recent rejections and their evidence of the world's indifference. All those vague notions we have about acceptance and success may be unrealistic and childish, but which of us ever outgrows them altogether?

Dickey, of course, had then, and has now, a paradoxical reputation. A roarer, a liar, a drunk, and a braggart, he was also an estimable poet. He could be a lout, and often was, in public. He could also do quirky things in private—like writing this letter. I didn't raise the question with Adrien, who was enjoying the comfort that his letter had brought her, but I did wonder whether Dickey might not have had an established policy of writing such letters to all the losers of all the prizes and awards for which he'd been one of the committee members, converting resentment and enmity into gratitude and friendship, not even because he particularly valued the friendship or intended to ask for favors but just because it was amusing to him to do things like this.

It wouldn't have been entirely beyond him. And even if this were a part of some manipulative game, who was hurt by it? Adrien was surely helped and encouraged.

Shortly after she received this letter, within a couple of weeks, I think, she died. And a month or two later, Jim Dickey showed up at the University of Pennsylvania to do a reading. I was a lecturer there in the English department, an adjunct, treated rather better than many of my fellow writers, but still a second-class citizen, paid less, and with no benefits, and without ever having been told this, destined to be let go after six years lest I begin to imagine myself a candidate for tenure. It was—and almost certainly still is—the way the department there treats writers, a necessary but nasty part of the business of literature. Writers are to English professors as aphids are to ants.

Barbarian though he tried to be, Dickey was quick to pick up on clues and cues, and at the party after his reading in Robert and Joanne Lucid's apartment, he sat down beside me on the couch, put his arm around my shoulder, and talked to me as if we were old friends, not because we were all that close but because he could see that it was a way of annoying his hosts. He and I had met twenty-five years before, when I spent a year in Atlanta at Georgia Tech to see if I liked teaching (I didn't). We hadn't kept up really, but Dickey and I had both made our debuts in John Hall Wheelock's Poets of Today series. George Garrett, a good friend of mine, had also published his first book in that series, and Dickey and Garrett had been friends and colleagues at the University of South Carolina. Dickey and I had crossed paths once or twice, I think, at Hollins College.

But Dickey was putting on a show to put down the profs. Bob Lucid's life work was a biography of Norman Mailer, which he is presumably still working on and in which not even Mailer, himself, could be much interested anymore. I remember being in Mailer's apartment in New York when I was doing a piece about him for *Newsweek,* and when Norman Podhoretz showed up, Mailer greeting him, bellowing, "Ah, the clerk of American literature."

As far as Dickey was concerned, all these English department people were clerks of American literature. Or it could have been less intellectual than that, mere mischievousness. But it felt good for the guest of honor to be singling me out this way, whatever his motives. I told him that Adrien had recently died and mentioned to him how deeply moved she had been by his letter and how happy it had made her. I said that he'd done a very decent, very generous thing. He didn't have anything smart to answer. Just a simple, "I'm glad." And then, "Thank you for letting me know."

They say that no good deed goes unpunished, and I was both pleased and appalled to learn from Laura Nelson Baker that Adrien had left a small sheaf of poems that she wanted me to get published. Publishing poetry is not an easy thing to do, and as Adrien had learned all too well, there are rejections and rebuffs, to which one becomes more or less inured. But to have a dead friend's work rejected is more burdensome, more annoying and offensive. I tried various places and was dismayed to find out that, even among university presses, there is a kind of commercial instinct that obtains. A dead poet? Difficult to promote. (As if there were a whole lot of promotion that publishers do for poets!) Less fancifully, there was a feeling that these publications are career stepping-stones, and that the appearance of a slender volume from some university press has its real consequences in the efforts of the poet to get himself or herself promoted from assistant to associate professor at the University of Far Away. It was an odd way to think about these matters, but it had an irresistible kind of reasonableness. Nothing could do Adrien any good anymore. There was no indirect way for her to cash in on the publication. Conversely, there was no indirect harm these publishers could think they were doing her by "passing," which is the euphemism, after all, not only for rejection but also for death.

It took me a couple of years of fitful effort, and then I asked John Irwin, who runs the contemporary poetry program at the Johns Hopkins University Press, whether he'd be interested. And he said, yes, absolutely, send the manuscript on down. Irwin is a quirky, cranky guy who can be wrong about manuscripts—he has rejected the book of one friend of mine that won the Pulitzer Prize for poetry—but at least he's quick. My friend has mixed feelings about the experience: Irwin returned the manuscript in a week, which may have been brusque but was less of an inconvenience than the three- or six-month turnaround time of a lot of publishers. (I remember the late Seymour Lawrence, to whom I'd sent a book of poems, justifying his protracted delay by telling me, with his very expensively cured stutter perhaps betraying some unease: "But, David, p-p-p-poetry is n-n-never urgent.")

There weren't enough poems to make a whole collection, but at this stage, and with all three of her books of poems out of print, it made sense to do a New and Selected. Irwin was receptive to that. But to make up for the awkwardness of not having a live author who could "promote" the book, he wanted some heavyweight to do an introduction, which would be one step beyond the ordinary dust jacket blurb and might improve the prospects for sales at least to schools and libraries.

I offered to do the introduction, but Irwin rejected that. He wanted an "important" poet.

"How about Jim Dickey," I suggested after only a moment's thought.

Irwin said that Dickey would be fine.

I got Dickey's number from Garrett, called, explained what John Irwin wanted, and then asked whether Dickey would be willing to write a brief introduction to Adrien's posthumous volume.

He didn't even take time to think about it but immediately said, "Sure." And he did, promptly, produce a three-page introduction that was neither assertive nor preening, that called attention in deft and shrewd ways to Adrien's strengths of talent and vision, and that alluded to Adrien's difficulties at the end of her life:

> I think often of the woeful neglect of this woman, of the marvelous creative intellect that earned a living as a small-town librarian and, under various pseudonyms by writing children's books, mysteries, and travelogs, and of Adrien Stoutenburg's time spent, during her terrible battle with esophageal cancer, in various hospitals and intensive care units, full of life near its suffering close, the special life that only the dying have. From one of these she protested

> With the tube down my throat
> I could not tell them.

> Now is the time for telling. Now, and from now on.

Irwin brought out the book, *Land of Superior Mirages,* in 1986. The title is one of the many striking lines from "This Journey," which is a part of the title poem of her first volume:

> This is the land of superior mirages,
> distortions, dreams, repeated rainbows,
> false sunsets and deceptive sunrises,
> ships overturned yet serenely riding
> the high abyss as if to some anchor
> hung between Polaris and the Goat.

Nobody talks much about Adrien's work these days, or not in ways that I'd be aware of. But I have faith in the poems, and I have faith, too, in what I see as at least the possibility of happy accidents. Those poems that seemed to her to have gone nowhere had been important to me and had resonated in Dickey's head, too, enough so that, for whatever reason, he could write her that letter. That he and I should have been brought together that way shortly after her death was a coincidence, or a concinnity, which is a fancier word that implies that there may be some kind of order in the world, that events can rhyme the way words do to make what would be otherwise unremarkable suddenly important and memorable.

The poems leave our hands and go out to seek their fortune in ways we cannot imagine. Her excellent poems have been more fortunate than Adrien realized. A month or two later, and that letter of Dickey's would not have been in time. And I wouldn't have heard about it. Irwin's enthusiasm, which she never knew about at all, turned out to be important to the poems. They're out there, published, on library shelves, waiting for the notice of those clerks of literature or the even more valuable attention of the casual reader who stumbles upon them somehow and takes them to heart.

Ole Fred

POETRY READINGS ARE PROBLEMATIC. THE convention is that poetry is a vocal art and that the tradition goes back to the bards, jongleurs, minnesingers, and skalds who entertained the aristocrats after dinner. But there aren't many aristocrats around anymore, and the art itself has changed, so that the selection from one's work of what might go over viva voce is an invidious business. There is a live voice in the head, perhaps, but it sings or speaks to an audience quite different from the bookstore venue or the college lecture hall. And as if choosing weren't bad enough, there is also the temptation, for younger poets anyway, of writing for that putative audience, of making the gestures just a little larger, a little clearer, so that they'll have a fairer chance of understanding what the poem says on a single hearing.

And then the audience can turn out to be so poignantly minuscule as to seem like a divine reproach for that temptation—to which you did not, after all, succumb, but for which you feel guilty nonetheless because it did flicker across your consciousness when you were sitting there at your desk. The diminutive audience record is probably held by Bink Noll, a very talented poet who was deeply pleased to be invited back to Princeton, his alma mater, to do a reading and who showed up and got taken to dinner at one of the eating clubs by some graduate assistant who'd been deputized to act as his host. During dessert, the graduate assistant is said to have apologized profusely and to have explained that he was doing his dissertation on Camus— who was in New York and had agreed to allow him to come up from Princeton and drive him from his hotel out to Idlewild. Therefore, if you don't mind, the graduate assistant said, I'll introduce you, leave the check on the lectern, and duck out so I can get to New York and do this. He explained that he'd had the news too late to be able to find a substitute, and that, in any case, he'd been looking forward to making this introduction.

Noll was feeling fine, happy to be back at Old Nassau, and reportedly told his host that he was quite comfortable and understood entirely. But when they got to the lounge where the reading was supposed to take place, they found only two—count 'em, two—students, huddled together on one of the sofas near the lectern that had been set up at one end of the room. The graduate student abbreviated his remarks drastically, slipped the check onto the lectern, and darted out. Noll got up before the two students, cleared his throat, and read a poem, whereupon one of the students asked whether there was some kind of event going on here. They were trying to study for a physics test.

Noll said he wouldn't bother them further, ducked out, and went to the Nassau Inn for a stiff drink, having had an audience of either zero or, if you want to be strict about it, minus two, a number that would qualify for the Guinness book if they took note of such things.

Of course, we all know about small audiences. Or we do now. My first poetry reading, though, must have had . . . sixty? seventy people? Something like that. It was at the University of Virginia, and I was, at the time, working at *Newsweek*. I'd published my first book, *Suits for the Dead*, in Scribner's Poets of Today series, and George Garrett had invited me down to read. Not so much because of the book, but to pay me back, which is how these things often work.

Not that he owed me, really. I'd reviewed a couple of books of his in the magazine, where I was a very junior "swinger"—*Time* called them "floaters" but that sounds like a body in the harbor. When either Wilder Hobson or Robert Massie, the two regular book reviewers, was on vacation, I was assigned to fill in, and confronting the table with those huge piles of books, all of them competing for notice in our limited space, I'd picked up *The Finished Man,* Garrett's first novel, read a few pages, and then announced that, if there were no objections, I'd do a review. It was an altogether innocent pick, uninfluenced by any publicist's call or promotional material. I just looked at the dust jacket and read the first couple of pages, the way one might do in a bookstore. My judgment wasn't infallible. My first assignment, actually, was to take a look at Leon Uris's *Exodus* and write either a review or a memo explaining why *Newsweek* should ignore the book. I looked through it, appraised it by the standards I'd been taught at Yale and Columbia, and wrote the memo saying that we could skip this one—correct but wrong.

With Garrett, though, I was quite right, and I'd found a really good book, good enough so that, the next summer, when one of the reviewers was away, I was back in the book review office and recognized Garrett's name on a collection of short stories. This time I grabbed it eagerly and cheerfully wrote the review. Short reviews of good books are easy to do: you just quote a lot and let the writer's voice come through. All you need is a lead, a paragraph or two about who the author is, and a kicker, and you're home free.

The reviews were unsigned back then. And although management decided that it would be good to have the names of the reviewers attached to the critical pieces in the magazine (it didn't cost anything and it made the reviews look more serious), I resisted, not just as an assistant editor, which I was at the time, but as the unit chairman of the Newspaper Guild. I said that if anybody made any changes in the copy, the first thing to come off would be the writer's signature. I had no idea how heavily the *New Yorker* was edited, or how quixotic I was being, but that was the position I took. And the editors, who messed with the copy because, if they didn't, there wasn't a whole lot of point to their being there, backed down. Only after I left the magazine did the names appear at the end of reviews, and then, later, at the end of ordinary stories. Garrett, then, had no idea who it was up in New York who was picking him out for such attention, but I moved up and became the movie reviewer.

In one of those dead weeks in early January, when few new films are released and we had to fill up the space with features, I found myself doing a piece about novelists who were writing screenplays. Styron was doing one, I remember, and . . . George Garrett! Whom I called and interviewed, about a script he was writing for, I think, *The Young Lovers* for Samuel Goldwyn Jr. Garrett answered all my questions, but then, at the end of the phone call, asked if he could put a question to me. Could I find out who it was up there who had been reviewing books of his? That was easy, because I was the guy, and I told him so.

He confirmed that I was the same Slavitt as had published in the Scribner's series. And then he asked if I did poetry readings. Would I be interested in coming down to the University of Virginia?

Sure, why not? I was delighted. But also a little afraid of it. I'd never done this. And I felt a little like an impostor. I'd been writing, at least in part, so as not to be a *Newsweek* guy who used to write but a writer who happened to work at *Newsweek*. And my bluff was being called. I said I'd be happy to come.

Time passes. What I don't know—and don't find out about for years—is that during the couple of months that intervene, there's a peculiar interchange down at Virginia in which a couple of football players who get good grades in some lecture course that Garrett has taught come to thank him. These are huge, hulking guys who go on, I think, to play pro ball. And they're from New York, and they talk funny for Charlottesville, and teachers haven't treated them well. But Garrett has given one of them an A and one an A minus, and they show up to thank him, and to let him know that they're grateful, and that if anybody gives him any trouble, if he needs anybody leaned on, so to speak, all he has to do is let them know.

Garrett manages not to laugh—he has had five professional bouts as a middleweight boxer, after all—and he reassures them that there was a grader and that he had nothing to do with the high marks he is sure they earned. But they're not convinced. They say they understand that that's what he has to say. But the offer stands.

And they go away, and Garrett pours himself a drink and forgets about it.

But then, on the day of the reading, there they are, looming up on what they call down there "Mr. Jefferson's lawn," as if the founder had gone out for a cup of coffee and might be back at any minute. They greet Professor Garrett and say how nice it is to see him. And they remind him of their offer. Garrett shakes his head and is about to send them away, but then he remembers that there are these two young poets he's invited to read that afternoon. If they might perhaps persuade some of their friends to come, he'd be most grateful.

So they go around collaring people and asking whether they'd like to go to a poetry reading or have their faces smashed, and most of those who respond to this survey choose 1 or A. And Fred Chappell and David Slavitt have an enormous audience, eager and attentive—because those two galoots are there in the back to check—and clapping after each poem.

I don't remember much more about the reading except what I've heard. Richard Dillard records in a verse essay that alludes to this occasion his recollection that Chappell was wearing a clip-on bow tie and claimed that he "had yet to master / The art of the knot," and I guess he did, but I didn't notice it. I do remember that Henry Taylor and Richard Dillard were in the audience. And Garrett was there, of course. And Fred and I were the readers. The five of us have been friends for almost forty years now, and, with Kelly Cherry and Brendan Galvin, published *A New Pléiade,* in which each of us picked the poems of that poet whose name alphabetically followed his or her own.

I also remember that I thought Fred Chappell had done this before. He seemed to know what he was about and read and moved authoritatively. I remember worrying about the fact that his poems were very good. (How would mine compare, after all?)

What I didn't know until the party afterward was that this was his first reading, too, and he thought I was the experienced one, the confident veteran performer. When we each found out that this had also been the other's first experience at this kind of thing, we relaxed and laughed, and have been, ever since then, colleagues. I have been able to delight in his successes—his excellent books, and also, from time to time, the recognition that his excellence has brought him. He has won the Bollingen Prize, after all, even if more people know the work, or at least the name of John Ashbery, with whom he shared the prize that year, than know Chappell's. Indeed, the general impression, I fear, is that Ashbery won the prize and Fred was a kind of an afterthought, when, in fact, the reverse is true. Louis D. Rubin, Annie Dillard, and Richard Howard were on the committee that year, and the decision, I am reliably told, had already been made—to give the award to Chappell. But Howard said that Ashbery was dying, that this would be the last chance to give him the prize, and that he wouldn't survive to the next award, which is, I believe, biennial. Howard's information turns out to have been incorrect. But Ashbery is a New York poet, and Chappell is down there in Greensboro, which is a pleasant enough place but not quite the red-hot center of intellectual life, or at least not in the minds of the editors of the *New York Review of Books*. So Chappell, it is assumed, was the afterthought.

But who cares? There's no sense in worrying about the size of one's audience or the scale of one's reputation, not if these things depend on the intervention of grateful football players, corrupt judges, or angels carrying out the instructions of a god even more whimsical than Garrett. Indeed, the lesson for Fred and me that day was clear enough—that we should distrust an audience that was too numerous and enthusiastic. Seldom have I faced a crowd that big, but one occasion I remember with particular clarity was at Oklahoma State University at Stillwater, where almost a hundred eager poetry fans had assembled to hear me read. Or, more accurately, had assembled for the reading. That I happened to be the one up there at the lectern was almost irrelevant.

OSU is—or was, then—an MFA factory with an enormous writing program. This was not the result of any deliberation about the proper mission of higher education in Oklahoma but rather an unintended consequence of a provision by which any high school graduate in Oklahoma is guaranteed admission to the University of Oklahoma or Oklahoma State. There's no guarantee that they'll succeed, of course, or even that they'll last into their sophomore year, but they all have the right to show up and try. It's the English department, then, that gets to sort out who stays in a Dr. Mengele–like exercise called freshman composition. The regular English faculty hates doing this, and to spare themselves they have created this large graduate program in creative writing. Apparently, they have beaters out in the sierras and the bayous, the big cities and small towns, looking for short-story writers, poets, librettists, novelists, hopeful scribblers of any kind who will come to take a few courses in creative writing and, not altogether incidentally, teach a couple of sections of freshman comp to these youngsters who are called, not very affectionately, "goat ropers."

They don't get paid much to do this. And on their budgets, they drink beer when they can afford it, except at the department parties, when they get invited to the chairman's house and can guzzle the department's scotch and bourbon and gin and vodka until they can't even lie on the floor without holding on. The signal for this debauch, the Pavlovian bell, one might say, is the poetry reading, which immediately precedes the party. The quality of the bell ringing or the identity of the bell ringer is not of paramount importance to the salivating dogs.

Depressing? Of course, but not definitively devastating. I cannot say for certain that no one in the hall heard what I was reading or even that no one liked it or misapprehended what the poems were doing. The truth of the matter, though, is that I have been spoiled, that no reading can ever compare with that blessed occasion in Charlottesville when I read with Fred, heard and immediately understood how good he was, and felt the inspiriting challenge that such first-rate work as his ought to offer. What doesn't kill us makes us stronger.

I can't be sure, but I assume he must have read "February," a splendid poem in his first book, *The World between the Eyes*, about hog-killing time on the farm. It seems, at least at first, to be a simple narrative about the dreadful but necessary business of butchering a hog, and the point of view of much of the poem is that of the boy who is watching this, horrified and fascinated as the men go about their bloody business. Of course, what I see now is that the piece is also clearly about poetry and poetry readings, and that sly Ole Fred was every bit as knowing as I took him to be, even if he hadn't done this before. The turn at the end is deft and economical, but clear enough:

> And his bladder and his stomach sack! puffed
> Up and tied off and flung to the kids,
> Game balls, they bat them about,
> Running full tilt head down across the scattered yard.
> And then on a startled breeze
> The bladder's hoist, vaults high and gleams in the sunlight
> And reflects on its shiny globe
> The sky a white square
> And the figures beneath, earnest figures
> Gazing straight up.

After all, we're spilling our guts, as one says, and there they are in the audience, enjoying it and having fun. It is the kind of transcendent moment that only the finest of poets could bring off.

Thomas McAfee

WHENEVER I BOOT UP MY computer, there's a moment early on when the McAfee logo appears on the screen, letting me know that its virus protection program is working. Fleetingly, I think of the other McAfee, the poet who died in 1982 and who ought to be famous.

The requirements for fame in poetry are quizzical, even vulgar. What seems to attract attention isn't the quality of the work—otherwise, Henry Taylor, and Geoffrey Hill, and William Heyen, and Donald Finkel would be names that commonly appear on the front page of the *New York Review*. What counts, rather, seems to be a display of suffering, as Bill Moyers so tediously demonstrated in his mawkish series on PBS, *The Language of Life*. Cancer victims, those afflicted with AIDS or whose partners were so afflicted, suicides, members of minority ethnic groups, the insulted and injured of all kinds were on offer, for reasons that are not entirely obscure. Edmund Wilson's essay "The Wound and the Bow" had suggested that artistic expression comes from a psychic wound; the extension and reduction of that thesis suggest that instead of paying attention to the art, which may be difficult and demanding, we may look directly to the suffering, which is much folksier and less demanding, and feel a warm empathy for these poor tormented poets. This was how Time, Inc., has traditionally treated all writers, and they had an additional motive in that every one of their minions had an abandoned novel or play or sheaf of poems stashed somewhere in a filing cabinet, way in the back, behind the Jack Daniel's bottle.

What Plath, Sexton, and Lowell and Berryman have in common is that they were public sufferers, and their suffering became their subject, so that we could read and either approve of the poetry or, failing that, condescend to forgive their lapses on account of their pain. It may not be the ideal literary situation, but that's how it was and still is, and in that case, McAfee ought to be way up there, valued not only for his anguish but for the interesting and authentic way he expressed it in his three books of poems.

The most vivid image that comes to my mind, though, is not from any of his poems but from a story George Garrett told me about McAfee's first poetry reading. McAfee's father was a formidable man who raised bulls in Haleyville, Alabama, wherever the hell that is, and apparently was less than delighted by his son's announcement that he was going to be a poet. Still, if that was what the young man wanted to do, the father supposed that he ought to go at it with seriousness and determination. Through a friend, then, he arranged for his son's first appearance at some women's club in St. Louis. This wasn't anything Tom had asked for or was eager to do, but it would have been most awkward to back out, so he went.

Imagine, then, an auditorium full of women in Helen Hokinson hats, and at one end of the room a stage with a lectern, behind which stood a big black grand piano. There's an introduction and then . . . he's on. He comes walking out onto the stage, a tall, slender, almost wraithlike young man, and he looks out at the audience, grips the lectern, goes pale, feels sick, and in desperation, turns around. Nothing there but the grand piano with its innards yawning. He leans and vomits into the piano, closes the lid, and then, in an inspired Artaud moment, bows and exits.

Stage fright? Disgust? What some bonehead comp student once

called "low self of steam"? Who knows? But it's the zero grade of reading disasters, compared to which any other appearance any of us makes, before no matter how small an audience in no matter how depressing a venue, is . . . not so bad.

I met McAfee once or twice. The first time would have probably have been at the party at Hollins College (College, then; University now) for *The Girl in the Black Raincoat,* an anthology Garrett edited and in which we both appeared. And the last time was at Columbia, Missouri, at the University of Missouri, where I went out to read, mostly because it would be a chance to see McAfee, whose work I admired and whom I liked a lot. In fact, we never quite connected. McAfee had written to say how much he was looking forward to my visit. And I have no doubt that he was. But he was a drunk, and he had bad days, bad weekends, even bad weeks. I checked in at the Tigertown Motel, an odd, slightly down-at-the-heels place not far from the campus where he lived. (It has since been spruced up a bit and has changed its name, preposterously, to "The Tiger Columns.") As soon as I got in, I called him, but he wasn't answering the phone. I left messages at the front desk. And there were one or two messages back, about how he wasn't feeling well, maybe later, maybe tomorrow. . . .

Drunks are like that, I guess. But much of what I know about alcoholism I know from McAfee's poetry. More than Dylan Thomas, McAfee is the bard of the bottle, as he demonstrates in this early poem from *I'll Be Home Late Tonight,* which has remained with me over the years:

IN THE RED

> Q.: Why do elephants drink?
> A.: To forget

I see the herd of them—their ragged skin
Warring against the formal afternoon sky—
As they sit, like lumps, for cocktails to begin.
"I think back on each conjugal lie

I've told," they wheeze; and this is their party talk.
Their skin goes red from gray as the sun descends.

"Wouldn't it be tranquility-grand to walk
Innocent at dawn, fresh, and at loose ends?"

They drink themselves ad nauseam till three,
When a cynical moon throws a little light, to lunge home.
Guilty insomniacs in their misery
They squint, all trembling, into the jungle, alone.

We can see how it works. The machinery is on show, as it can be with some of those transparent watches, where you can watch the wheels go around and the back-and-forth of the escapement. The elephant, because of its size, is an object of pity—as in Edward Lear and T. S. Eliot. The trick of the light as the sun descends turns them from real elephants to the pink ones of delirium tremens, but not frightening. They still have their appeal, their modest, clumsy dignity, which is how he gets away with "tranquility-grand."

I can't remember what my reaction to the poem was before that two and a half days in Columbia and those messages at the desk of the Tigertown Motel. But since then, knowing that he was upstairs, that he was trembling, was sick, was ashamed, that he wanted to see me and, worse, knew I wanted to see him and had come a thousand miles mainly to spend a little time with him . . .

It breaks my damned heart.

According to the biographical material supplied on the Web by the library of the University of Missouri, where McAfee's papers are housed, he "succumbed to lung cancer on 10 August 1982 after a short stay at the Truman Veterans Hospital in Columbia. As per his instructions, his body was donated to the University School of Medicine for scientific research."

Talk about "Anatomy of the World," or "Anatomy of Melancholy." Here he is, the man stricken with cancer while he was busy drinking himself to death, who has published a novel, stories, and collections of poetry but still wants to show that he's good for something.

In that seedy motel lobby, there were fragmentary messages from him from upstairs somewhere. It is, I suppose, a perfectly persuasive representation of the relationship between writer and reader. I was downstairs, reading slips of paper McAfee had dictated to the desk clerk; I'm still downstairs, but now the messages are the poems, slightly more elaborate, but with the same shame and pain:

INTRODUCTION TO THE DRAMA

There must be balloons dropping
From a ceiling
Where noise is, festive.
I remind myself, these
Provinces aren't the world.
Here it looks and feels
Like Shakespeare's winter.
An old man in the hotel
Lobby says triumphantly,
"It's August." He shouts
So he can hear himself, and
He's forgotten his teeth
Again.
            How can I answer?
Tell him discontent is in
The corners? Tell him
The mezzanine is full
of discontent?
                It's five
O'clock in the morning,
Where somewhere parties
Are at their height. Men
Goosing women. Everybody
Wild with booze. The balloons
Going off like rifle shots.
Dancing. Everybody dancing.

His friends in Columbia were Bill and Margaret Peden and Larry Levis, who were helpful to him (now that I think of it, Bill

Peden was the one who arranged my visit, and Larry Levis introduced me at my reading) and whom McAfee treated—he couldn't
help it—the way he treated me. There's a scary poem in which he
confesses this:

LEAVING TOWN
for Mark Strand

When I leave town, everybody
Leaves town. The Pedens may still
Be here buying light bulbs at Skaggs
And the Levises eating shrimp with
        lobster sauce
        at Kai Min.

But I am out of town, hidden
In a dead womb, shut off, shut down,
Shut away in black blood.

I come back, and it is good to come back,
To say to Larry Levis,
"How do you open this door
To this car
To get to the party we're going to?"

Drinking isn't McAfee's only subject, but it comes up a lot. Indeed, it is almost assumed, so that sobriety is the remarkable and not
altogether desirable condition, as in this one, from *I'll Be Home Late
Tonight:*

ZONE OF QUIET DESPERATION
headline from Saturday Review, *October 10, 1964*

I won't confess anything—
to sweetheart or priest or friend.
I've got a man stored inside
to the terrible end.
        He listens

and won't talk back.
But he's a damn sore tooth,
a heart attack, a loss of breath . . .
He's—what can I tell you?—
the dreary end
of the benefit.
He's when you're sober.
He's the imperative.

More often, there are glancing references to what is the normative
landscape, as in "Because There Is So Much Weather in My Mind,"
in which, when someone asks him if he's been sick, he explains his
pallor by saying:

I've sat all night in air conditioned bars
And slept all day with sleeping pills
In air conditioned hotel rooms. I've turned
Away from the rainy windows of
Royal Street and matched the stoned
Bartender for another drink.
The gin does nothing, and I decline
His fist of red pills. In Manhattan
The nasal twang of a native
Reminds me of hot Sunday afternoons
In Mississippi and Alabama.
The expensive beaches she waits
All year for—theirs is the sun
That sets on fire the Alabama red dust
And agonizes my mind and leaves cancer
Under the movie star tan.

He is not his only subject. There are quick sketches that remind
me of T. S. Eliot's vignettes in *The Waste Land* or, more accurately,
suggest what the poems might have been like if Eliot hadn't left Missouri and gone off to England. Back in Missouri, in "Translating in
Brazil," a late, long, very impressive poem, McAfee writes:

> The woman sprawled
> On her back porch late in the afternoon.
> Her legs aren't shaved. "I don't care," she says
> As she drinks beer from a can. "If he's in
> That bitch, let him look at my hairy legs."
> Mrs. Watson nods but doesn't agree. All the time,
> Sun is seeping through trees, preparing a scene
> For distance.
>   Now we have a scene and mystery.
> No voice. The woman and Mrs. Watson are there,
> Pencil sketches. They have been dead for years.
> The woman did shave her legs. Mrs. Watson
> Moved to Detroit and lived a terrible life.

The ruthless intrusion of aestheticism in the observation about the sun, "seeping through trees, preparing a scene / For distance" reminds us that we're not there to help them or even to offer sympathy, but are reading a poem, which demands the heartlessness and precision—the "distance"—that McAfee understood was fundamental to the practice of art. Here is the very opposite of Moyers's inclusive vulgarity. Which is, of course, the answer to the question with which I began. That's exactly why he's not famous.

It must have been pretty bad in that room above the lobby. The messages he sent down to me were terse and regretful. The messages continue to arrive. A little later in that same poem, there's an amazing passage:

> In this room, I see an elephant coming towards me. He's
> Somewhere in Africa. He's determined. I can tell. His ears
> Flare like flowers. He won't harm me. He'll go through me
> And the wall and come back again from the other wall.
> Without fear, I look down. I light a cigarette. I study
> My fingernails and the ring on my finger. Easily, I
> Accept the elephant. I welcome him. Sometimes, when
> I go astray, I wonder why he's alone.

It's Rimbaud, but without all that French nonsense, or Hart Crane
without the Life Savers. He could do amazing things and was getting
better and better. Like van Gogh.

I'll let him have the last word, the ending of "Back for the Last
Funeral: The Stations" in which he says:

And

Afterwards, there was no passenger train
To take him back to the city. No airport.

The cemetery still in his eyes, he waved goodbye
From the Greyhound bus. And I waved and knew
I had already seen the last of him a long time ago.

Richaleh:
Richard Elman

I KNEW RICHARD ELMAN: WE were friends.

But how well did I know him? How friendly were we? We had some experiences in common, and we entertained each other. It was a pleasure for each of us to make the other laugh and to be immediately understood. (Isn't that what all writers want, after all? Isn't that why we became writers?) But we didn't spend a lot of time together.

I read, while he was alive, some of his fiction, much of his reportage, and most of his poetry. I can feel guilty about that, if I'm in a mood for self-laceration. A friend owes a friend more than that. But now that he is dead, I am atoning, going through his work in a systematic way in order to write about him, and only now do I see what I ought to have seen and understood before—the magnitude of his talent and the meagerness of the rewards it brought him.

He was a funny fellow, but a sense of humor is often depression's handmaiden. Both as a writer and as a teacher, he was a connoisseur of disappointment. It was his lot, his karma, and he was a master of it. (The alternative would have been unattractive—to let it be the master of him.) Let me offer a couple of examples:

Elman at Newsweek: We were there together in the late fifties. I worked there for seven years and he for maybe seven weeks. And each of us, as we later discovered, admired the other's career. He thought it was a demonstration of my doggedness and virtue that I put up with the magazine for so long in order to earn a living and support my wife and children. I thought it was a sign of his refinement that he was unable to endure its lower-middle-brow limitations and Dilbert-like demands. But it wasn't until years later that I learned the details of his separation from his employment there.

On a Friday evening, word came through that there had been a coup d'état in Madagascar. This is, in the world of weekly newsmagazines, the worst time for anything to happen, because the issue is going to bed but they have to take note of some world event. (Or that's what it was like back then, in the fifties, before the twenty-four-hour news cycle.) Some senior editor pulled Elman off whatever he was doing and told him to go and write background about Madagascar—a Kafkaesque assignment because it was late enough so that there were no places to go, nothing to work from except the meager resources of *Newsweek*'s own library, which is to say the usual set of encyclopedias and almanacs. I doubt that they'd have had a lot in the files about Madagascar. But it was a crisis and the senior editor wasn't in the mood to entertain complaints or protests. Elman sat at his desk, thinking about the lunacy of his situation, and he responded with the lunacy it seemed to demand, typing out utter nonsense about an imaginary Madagascar, a generic if fictive place that set decorators for B movies might have imagined. Clackety-clack (there were still typewriters back then).

And at a certain point, someone came by to take away the sheaf of pages he had produced and, before Elman could warn him that nothing he had written was of any earthly use (not on this earth, anyway), he was gone. Eventually, the writer putting the story together from the wire service reports and whatever else he'd been supplied with glanced at what Elman had done, and his eye lit on something attractive, which appeared in the story, in the penultimate paragraph, the suggestive but altogether meaningless remark Elman had brought back from his trek through the mental jungle: "When the flute plays in Madagascar, East Africa dances."

On Monday, both delighted and appalled to see that this fortune cookie slogan had made it into the magazine, he told someone—the writer? the editor? some fellow sufferer he thought he could trust?— that this had been a sheer fabrication, utter nonsense, and that it was a joke that it had been printed. A joke, yes, but the butt was Elman, who was, that very day, summarily dismissed.

And a couple of days later, looking through the *New York Times*, which he'd bought for the classified ads because he needed a job, he noticed, on the editorial page, in a discussion of the recent events in Africa, an allusion to the "well-known proverb" that tells us how "when the flute plays in Madagascar, East Africa dances."

Elman at Penn: It's decades later, and Elman is now at the University of Pennsylvania, an adjunct lecturer who schleps down from Stony Brook, where he lives and has tried but failed to get a job at SUNY's Stony Brook campus. He has to take the LIRR to Penn Station, change to an Amtrak train, come to Philadelphia, and then walk to Bennett Hall where he is badly paid—but, still, paid something— by an English department that offers a writing program but has never felt it necessary or even relevant to hire any full-time writers.

Elman hoped to work his way into a full-time appointment. At the very least, he hoped that the gig might be repeated. He needed the money, after all. And he was a good teacher, helping these kids learn to read and write, which is, or ought to be, the main job of an English department. (What he didn't know was that the department never keeps writers around for very long, thinks of them as disposable, and doesn't want them even to imagine themselves getting raises or such unwriterly fripperies as medical coverage.) Quite late in the term, he was informed that his services would not be required for the following year. He was—quite justifiably—furious, but, as he told me one afternoon, he managed to extract a kind of poetic justice, if not actual revenge. What he'd done was to go to the chairman of the department and announce that he was leaving teaching to go back to his first love, which was cooking. He'd accepted a job at Lutèce as a vegetable cook. But he needed a small favor—a reference. "I've never had the pleasure of cooking for you," he'd told the chairman, "and I don't expect you to vouch for my culinary abilities. But if you could tell them that I'm sober and honest, that'd be a great help."

He smiled and, after a moment, I understood. Sober? Honest? The chairman was widely known to have a problem with alcohol. And I also remembered having heard—in Elman's presence, actually—a story about how, many years before, that same chairman had been suspected of having taken a typewriter belonging to a friend of ours. But with some earnestness and in not quite sufficient chagrin, this drunk, who was also quite possibly a thief, had offered to vouch for Elman's sobriety and honesty.

"And there's one more thing," Elman told me he'd said to the chairman. "They don't know I've been teaching. They think "The English Department" is the name of a restaurant here in Philadelphia. So when people answer the phone, it'd be good if they could find out who's calling before they let on that this is part of a university. . . ."

This time, a big smile, an ear-to-ear grin, because we both knew that the department *wasn't* a department and that Penn wasn't a real university, but only a sham, a con, a not quite convincing simulacrum.

I did a turn there, too, was as brusquely let go, and thought of Elman and the truth of those almost audible quotation marks he had managed to insert around "The English Department" with which the secretaries answered the telephone and which, for me, will always be there.

As will the books, or some of them. There are others I haven't read and probably won't but of which it is important, nevertheless, to take note. Badges of honor, they are, or at least Purple Hearts from the literary campaigns. I am looking at the bibliography and a few of the items require at the least some mention. *Taxi Driver,* for instance, a "novelization" written "with Paul Schrader," and published by Bantam Books in 1976. This was a hack job Elman undertook out of desperation. He wrote the "novelization," the paperback souvenir of the Martin Scorsese film. And there were scenes in it that were good enough for Schrader, the screenwriter, to say that he wished he could have used them. Mark Weiss, his friend and publisher (of *Cathedral-Tree-Train and Other Poems*), tells me that it has "some of Richard's best and most powerful writing" and that after some agonizing, Elman decided that he had to sign it with his own name. Contractually, Elman had to share writing "credit" with the author of the screenplay, but there was no reciprocity, despite the truth of what had happened. There was no such temptation for *Smokey and the Bandit,* a novelization of that dim Burt Reynolds/Jackie Gleason comedy written under the pseudonym of "Delmar Hanks" (which I take to be an anagram of "Rhd. Elman's A.K."). How does that comport with the bright promise of his first publication, *A Coat for the Tsar,* which came out in Harry Ransom's *Texas Review* and then was published by the University of Texas Press? That was, if anyone remembers, the big time back then, and, with big oil money, they were publishing such writers as Robert Graves, Samuel Beckett, Frank Lloyd Wright, Aaron Copland, Edward Steichen, Robert Penn Warren, Allen Tate, John Wain, J. B. Priestley, Angus Wilson, W. H. Auden, Stephen Spender, Marianne Moore, Octavio Paz, Eudora Welty, Katherine Anne Porter, Ignazio Silone, Jorge Luis Borges, and Lyndon B. Johnson. Some numbers of the magazine offered blocks of articles devoted to single topics, and supplements were later issued as books, among them the *Centennial Celebration of Baudelaire's "Les Fleurs du Mal";* George Garrett's second book of poems, *The Sleeping Gypsy;* and Richard Elman's *A Coat for the Tsar.* It was classier and lots more serious than the *New Yorker.* And that's where he started, a kid, twenty-four years old, hot, a comer who had studied at Stanford (with Yvor Winters and Malcolm Cowley). In the next few years, he went on to publish with Scribner's—five novels, a book of short stories, and a book of reportage about the Rolling Stones. Scribner's then was a first-line house, and when Burroughs Mitchell, his editor there, retired and wrote his memoirs, Elman's was one of the names he would drop of important writers he'd published during his long and illustrious career. But then come the tie-in paperbacks of movies and even TV shows (*Gangster Chronicles,* a TV tie-in, written under the pseudonym of Michael Lasker, with Richard A. Simmons [Jove, 1981]). Heartbreaking, heartbreaking. . . .

The key book, I think, of the whole oeuvre is *Fredi & Shirl & the Kids,* which calls itself a novel, but qualifies that in the subtitle, *The Autobiography in Fables of Richard M. Elman* (in *Name Dropping,* Elman calls it frankly and less complicatedly his autobiography). The connections between fiction and real life are not very tenuous. The names of his relatives are changed but only slightly, so that Eddie and Pearl, his real parents, are transformed to Fredi and Shirl, while brother Lenny becomes brother Benny. Richard, of course, remains Richard. The book begins:

> We played three or four neighborhoods in Brooklyn, a country house along the Jersey Shore, a number of relative parties, occasional requests from The Clients: Fredi & Shirl & The Kids. A family. Straight! Like a jab. Everybody on the block knew us. Some were more or less like us. Intimacies as crass as a grab, or a poke. A straight family type affair.
> A miracle. Fredi & Shirl, Bennett & Richard, all the same flesh: a lawyer, a housewife, an older brother. Hey, what about me?
> Bennett says, WRETCHED RICHARD.
> Fredi says, LITTLE MR. RICHARD.
> Shirl says, MY LITTLE RICHALEH.
> Show business is learning to get along with people.
> *   *   *
> RICHALEH . . .
> Ma! Bleating back, Ma! . . .
> An oxen calf, a dullard.
> Why not hit him over the head with a mallet?
> IF YOU DON'T BEHAVE YOURSELF MR. RICHARD I WILL . . .
> A neat vaudeville turn: Fredi has just thrown me head first against the radiator with one hand at age three and a half because I interrupted his perusal of the Sunday *Times.*

> The trouble one takes to get one's children's heads stitched.
> Why do we suffer bores so gladly?
> Tradition—a pageant of begats and begats.
> BIG FAT BULLY!
> THIS IS YOUR MOTHER SPEAKING RICHARD. WHAT
> DID YOU HAPPEN TO CALL YOUR OWN FATHER?
> MR. HITLER THE BULLY!
> YOU OUGHT TO BE ASHAMED OF YOURSELF. MR.
> RICHARD . . . ALL THE TROUBLE YOU'VE CAUSED . . .
> *WHAT* ABOUT *HIM?*
> YOUR FATHER REALLY LOVES YOU RICHARD. SURE
> HE DOES . . .
> SHIRL TELL THAT LITTLE KID OF YOURS TO SHUT
> UP!

The abuse, alas, was not a fiction. What it can do is drive a child inward, so that he retreats from an irrational and intolerable external world in which the father hits and the mother, who professes love, fails nevertheless to protect her child. Having nowhere else to go, he resorts to fantasy. He contrives an altogether useless distinction between his father, Fredi, the lawyer, and the one he is not afraid to blame—Mr. Strap.

If it doesn't make you crazy, it can make you a writer.

"Mr. Hitler" sounds like a piece of hyperbole, but in the late thirties and early forties, Hitler was not merely a political and historical but also a mythological presence. As Fredi says, a few pages later, "LISTEN MR. RICHARD. I WANT YOU TO BEHAVE YOUR-SELF . . . OR ELSE THERE'LL BE TROUBLE FOR ALL OF US. I'LL TELL HITLER ALL ABOUT YOU AND THEN HE'LL COME OVER HERE AND HE'LL COME AND GET YOU . . ." Shirl warns Fredi not to say such things that are likely to frighten the boy, but that, of course is "Precisely what Fredi had in mind. All during the war years I slept with the covers over my head so Hitler wouldn't come and get me."

The battle of Stalingrad is going on and, as the narrator points out, "My father wants to knock me from pillar to post. Stalin says, fight to the death. Hitler says, fight to the death. Fredi says he wants to tear me limb from limb. I wonder who is going to win this war."

Where it gets to is not, after all, so far-fetched:

SOMETIMES I HOPE HITLER WINS.
ZUGNISHT. [Yiddish for an emphatic "Don't say such a thing."]
HE'LL KILL US AND THEN WE'LL ALL BE DEAD.
SHIRL DID YOU HEAR WHAT THAT LITTLE KID OF YOURS JUST SAID?
Shirl turns around and says, RICHARD IF HE DOES I PROMISE YOU'LL NEVER FORGET IT.

And, of course, he doesn't. Indeed, that odd bit of psychodrama is the ore Elman mines for his Eastern European trilogy, *The Twenty-eighth Day of Elul, Lilo's Diary,* and *The Reckoning,* about the Yagodah family in Clig, in Hungary, where until quite late in the war the Jews thought they were safe and might survive. The piecemeal diminution of their freedoms and their prospects made for an exquisite prolongation of their sufferings unlike those of other European Jews, and their temporizations and accommodations to the Nazi threat were particularly nightmarish in the way the victims were forced to cooperate in their own humiliation and destruction. Not surprisingly, Newman Yagodah, the paterfamilias, is also a lawyer, an arrogant and opinionated man, not stupid so much as actively wrongheaded in his views. When the narrator's Uncle Bela writes from the States about Kristallnacht, the family contrives to rationalize, believing that "the Jews of Germany had brought disaster on themselves—by intermarriage, the assimilation, by aping the gentiles. That was the extent of our Jewish identity: we were critical of others but remained opportunistic and quite optimistic when it came to our own situations. None of us would have thought of marrying a Hungarian (because the women were all said to be whores and the men all cruel) but, as we wished to continue to do business—and that necessitated being neighborly—we disregarded Bela's letters and went about our business."

It was a curious project for an American Jew to undertake, and

Elman's choice of a subject can be explained in perfectly rational ways. The Shoah was a hallmark event, not only of his time but of our hideous century. Still, I can see how little Richaleh's tormented fantasies could have provided a part of the impetus for such an ambitious undertaking—a novel about a time and place with which Elman was not familiar, or at least not in its external details. The inner workings of the betrayal of the Yagodahs by the rapacious gypsy, Skirzeny, were familiar enough. The Yagodahs live in a mansion that once belonged to Skirzeny, for whom the government's anti-Semitism turns out to be not at all inconvenient. Eddie Elman, Richard's father, was a lawyer whose clients included a number of automobile junkyards and used-parts dealers. These people may not all have been crooks, but they had about them a coarseness and a menace that impressed the lawyer's son, and that turned out to be contagious. Elman told me once that his father habitually carried startlingly large rolls of bills in his pocket (these clients of his ran all cash businesses and always paid fees—or bail, or bribes—in cash.

Whatever the difference in scale of external events, the domestic characterizations would not have been altogether unknown to Elman, who writes, in Alex Yagodah's voice:

> The honest man of affairs became a murderer. You could see it in the way he walked. Father's crime was implicit in every one of his gestures from that day on, as if he had felt a sudden blow across the legs. My poor father. . . . I suppose Mother was more fortunate because she had always been allowed to seem the weaker of the two, and had her supposed weakness to disguise herself; when Father began to play his little tune Mother did not dance with the rest of us. She surrendered to a yielding, a softness, to frequent outflowings of tears, fits, brief moments of naked unguarded hysteria, the final diminution of her person. Whereas Father slowly crumbled from within himself, corroded and consumed by his own complicity, Mother merely wept when she was spoken to, keeping her feelings that way at an arm's distance from herself.

Skirzeny is arranging the Yagodahs' escape, but his price keeps escalating—what choice has Newman Yagodah, after all, but to pay

whatever is asked? Finally, the Gypsy demands Lilo (Lise Lotte
Gero, Newman's pretty niece and ward and Alex's beloved). She
must remain behind with Skirzeny and his all but feral stepson, Mik-
los, who has already raped her. It is an unspeakable bargain. But they
make it, and are, of course, betrayed anyway.

But there is, I think, in that ultimate wretchedness and brutality
the Yagodahs suffer something that spoke to the author, something
unimpeachably authentic and recognizable for a man who had once
cowered under the covers in dread of Mr. Hitler and Mr. Strap during those years of his childhood in a charade of middle-class respectability every bit as fragile as that of the Hungarian Jews.

There were other, subtler ways in which Elman's struggle with his
father manifests itself in his Hungarian trilogy. He freely admits, in
Namedropping, in his essay about Isaac Bashevis Singer, that in his late
twenties and early thirties, he hung around with the great Yiddish
writer who was not then anywhere near so celebrated as he would
later become. He was, as he puts it, "looking for a master," and came
"to declare [him]self his devoted protégé,"—or, as he later describes
it, rather more harshly, his "epigone,"—but what Elman eventually
discovered was that Singer "was not quite interested in me."

It was not a rejection, but, given Elman's early hurts, it may have
been worse and, paradoxically, just what he was looking for. They
spent a fair amount of time together. "So much of what he repre-
sented had been turned to ashes, though not Singer, who had escaped
that fate to be my teacher, not only through his writing but through
his conversation about his life in Warsaw, his friends and lovers,
though not about the child of love he'd abandoned to escape to
America." That Singer was a bad father only made him all the more
attractive to the hurt young man, and Singer's self-absorption, which
Elman recognized and describes in his essay, was tantalizing and, in
the root sense, familiar. "Bashevis," he writes, "never complimented
me except in odd ways: 'You have good color today.' I thought that
was because he did not really enjoy my company or my conversation.
He also had nothing good to say about any other writer I claimed to
find interesting. Jean-Paul Sartre was not 'a good writer,' he told me
when the Frenchman was awarded the Nobel Prize and "Babel was a
Marxist until it killed him.'" Elman then remarks that "It's probably

no accident that living in the middle of the city I chose to write my
first extended fictions through various central European mouth-
pieces; there were in such books . . . as *The Twenty-eighth Day of
Elul* parodic elements abstracted from the careful, accented speech of
Bashevis."

Although the first volume is an extraordinary tour de force, an amazing achievement for an American, the trilogy does not sustain itself.
Singer himself never attempted such a representation of the approach of the Shoah, choosing—out of caution, shrewdness or, conceivably, even modesty—to imply what he could by showing those
who had survived and escaped and what it had done to them. It is the
huge horror that looms ahead of some of the characters in the stories
set in Poland or that stains the past, having wrecked the lives of those
we see behaving so strangely in the Bronx and Brooklyn and Florida
in *Enemies: A Love Story* and *Shadows on the Hudson*. Elman doesn't
try to show us the agony directly, either, but imagines its approach
and invokes it as the background for what is after all a sordid domestic drama. The first novel was successful enough for Burroughs
Mitchell to encourage or at least allow Elman to continue with *Lilo's
Diary* (1968) and *The Reckoning* (1969), but as the Yagodahs became
more real to him, they became less useful as vehicles for discharging
the energy of his displaced rage. That wellspring of emotion he
would tap into again in *An Education in Blood* (1971), in which there
are clear similarities between the author and Stephen Tolmach, a
journalist ("the name is almost but not quite Hamlet" if one spells it
backward) who is writing about Bernard Eastover, who may or may
not have been guilty of the murder, thirty years before, of his wife.
That horrible incident in which he was thrown against a radiator
makes its first appearance here:

> *And then he remembered his father's upraised hand and the cold trickle
> against his forehead when, at age three or four, Stephen had been
> dashed against a radiator in a fit of rage by this brutal, ambitious,
> childlike man over the way his life was racing toward an empty
> grave . . .*

The novel is sadly dated: its combination of Herbert Gold's wise guy hipsterism with self-indulgent literariness may have been modish at the time but now it makes for tough going. None of that was Elman's voice, anyway, and what seems remarkable is that he could have persuaded himself into such strained and unnatural locutions. It was in his next book, *Fredi & Shirl & the Kids* (1972), that he found a way to bring his wry humor to bear on the outrages that remained his subject. Understated and faux-naïf, he could talk more directly about what his childhood had been like and show us where his rebelliousness and social and political contrariness came from. (He was always a leftist, but his clear-sightedness got him into trouble even with those with whom he ordinarily would have been allied. That he hated the Samocistas never blinded him to the book burning and other such lapses of the Sandinistas, whom he took to calling unreconstructed Stalinists.)

Fredi & Shirl & the Kids is not yet a perfect book. It loses some of its charge as Elman gets to his college days at Syracuse, by which time his protagonist is less and less the victim and, increasingly, the collaborator in the varieties of his own undoing. But it is authentic Elman, funny, angry, quirky, and occasionally sweet, and I recognize in it, particularly in the first half, the man I knew. It cost him a lot. His father never talked to him again (and at her death, his mother left him only a quarter of her estate, most of the rest going to his brother, with whom, nevertheless, Richard managed a rapprochement). It is the last of his Scribner's novels. There is a book of short stories that they publish in 1973, and, that same year, a piece of reportage, *Uptight with the Rolling Stones: A Novelist's Report* that had run in a shorter form in *Oui*, but by 1976, he's got that Bantam Books paperback original novelization of *Taxi Driver* and in 1978, his name is so much a liability that he and his editor decide that it might be a good idea to use a pseudonym for his next novel, *Little Lives* (by John Howland Spyker).

Now there's nothing inherently wrong with the use of pseudonyms. They can be ways of distinguishing among one's books. C. Day Lewis and Gore Vidal, when they wrote mysteries, were Nicholas Blake and Edgar Box. I've used pseudonyms myself at various times and for various reasons, mostly in an attempt to avoid confusion between my higher- and lower-brow audiences. But with the

Elman/Spyker book, a quirky series of sketches in the manner of
Sherwood Anderson, or, say, John Aubrey, of the inhabitants of a
small town in upper New York State, there are other indications of
difficulty. Evidently, neither editor nor author ever proofread the
text, which is in deplorable shape. It is unsettling to notice that names
can be spelled in different ways as they recur and to come across such
a sentence as: "She had a carriage with a pair of white horses that she
kept beplumed, and a her coachman in his livery boasted of the col-
ors of the Italianate Savoy."

Such a passage is not one that anyone writes. It is written off.
Elman's difficulties are not difficult to imagine. His career, which had
started out with such promise, wasn't going well. To some degree, he
blamed the Hungarian trilogy which, because it refused to make the
victims of the Shoah more heroic than they probably were, offended
a lot of New York tastemakers. One can follow the decline in the bibliography: Grosset and Dunlap was not a first-line house. (I know: I
published a book there, too.) And Elman, in the words of one of his
editors, "savaged all of those who supported him." Whatever the
world gave him, "he always wanted more," which may have been
justifiable and even reasonable but was hardly endearing. He didn't
have an agent but dealt with publishers directly, and he wasn't easy.
From Grosset and Dunlap, he went to other hack jobs—*Smokey and
the Bandit* (Bantam) and *Gangster Chronicles* (Jove). But he was by no
means played out.

Cocktails at Somoza's, which came out from Applewood Books in
1981, is a fine work, an impressive piece of reportage that transcends
genre so that, as one reads it now, it is quite simply literature. I can
think of only a few passages by Hemingway or even Tolstoy that are
as good at this kind of detailed, understated presentation of the rav-
ages of war:

> From the village square came the sound of firecrackers going off,
> many at a time, and I recognized that spattering noise, so different
> from gunfire, for exactly what it was, as I recalled one of the sieges
> of Masaya when the rebels had surrounded the Guard *cuartel* in
> August, 1978 and had set off firecrackers to simulate the noise of
> the automatic weapons they then lacked.

They had failed that time, and so many had died. Yet in Masaya, yesterday, as we walked the streets, my friend Marco introduced me to everybody as "Richard, a writer; *he* helped us!"

Although I hadn't really been comfortable with such an introduction, it was also true that I wasn't enjoying this perfect lack of human contact either. Why had I come to La Paz today? What had I wanted?

This is quite early in the book, and he finds that connection he is looking for, in the bed of a Toyota pickup in which he gets a ride back to Managua. The driver is bringing back the corpse of his wife's cousin so that his *compañeros* can rebury him. Elman tries his best but can't stand the smell of "that heap of heroic maggots" opposite him. He gets out and waits for a bus to take him back to the capital city.

It is *témoignage* honest enough to admit its powerlessness and even its irrelevance. And there are admissions of Elman's own emotions and politics that make Hemingway's taciturnity about such matters seem willful and mannerist. In one of the passages he quotes from his diaries, he reports:

> The prisoner knelt on the floor of the little wooden shed where we had been detained by two armed Guardsmen for taking photographs.
>
> He had been hit hard many times in the face before we came into the room, and deep reddish-bluish marks stood out on his otherwise pale cheeks.
>
> His lips were very red, as if he'd been rouged, but so were those of his frightened whimpering girlfriend: a dark plump girl in a purple blouse who stood in a corner, weeping.
>
> He was made to turn out his pockets. Then he was asked to stand up and an officer of the National Guard felt among his calves for weapons and then undid his trousers and searched all around his privates roughly and with his bare hands.
>
> There were a couple of other Guardsmen in the room, and two plainclothes paramilitaries bearing Uzis.
>
> The prisoner's girlfriend wept and wept. Her fear itself seemed

voluptuous, the aftermath of their arrest when they had been caught necking in a place they should not have been, and were believed to be Sandinistas.

It wasn't clear to me who they were just then, but I thought they probably would be Sandinistas soon, to judge from the boy's face, narrow, angular, and pale, bruised, with one of the eyes half-closed. That face was pushed forward slightly throughout the brutal interrogation so that the slightest touch against his person registered as grave injuries to his self-esteem.

I can't imagine Hemingway writing that essential phrase—"but I thought they probably would be Sandinistas soon"—which is, in Elman's practice, both a part of the scene and an admission, or assertion, of the fact that he was there.

He records his thereness in other ways, too, which is reasonable enough, given that complicated people have various modes and levels of engagement. What enlivens *Cocktails at Somoza's* and makes it all the more appealing is the humor of it, the recognition that the *norteamericano periodista,* however sympathetic, is a citizen of the country that is, in large measure, responsible for the outrages that are everywhere evident. The rage and the humor coexist and, indeed, feed each other, and it is in *The Breadfruit Lotteries,* written roughly at the same time, where the comedy predominates. The great difference between Nicaragua and Jamaica is that the latter, where *The Breadfruit Lotteries* is set, isn't serious or blood soaked. John Leonard was close enough when he observed in his *New York Times* review that it is "as if Lenny Bruce had written a James Bond" novel.

Actually, it seems to me more like Graham Greene or Eric Ambler, with the almost innocent protagonist getting himself enmeshed in the complications of espionage and assassination. Robert Harmon is a professor of political science at Columbia—Elman was an adjunct there too for a while—who goes to Jamaica essentially on a vacation with Dyllis Harwell, his second-best graduate student. There he gets recruited by the KGB, Mossad, and the CIA, and absurd things happen to him that are not, actually, much sillier than much of what probably goes on in the Caribbean. *The Breadfruit Lotteries* is by no means a great book, but it is entertaining, and, in a purely literary way, interesting. My guess is that from his experience with these hackwork jobs of novelization, Elman had learned how to move a story forward briskly and efficiently, working his reversals and revelations, and if his characters and their situation sometimes seem a bit cartoonish, it is a self-aware kind of cartooning, closer in spirit to the work of Roy Lichtenstein than that of Milton Caniff.

The reviews were good. After John Leonard's enthusiastic notice in the daily *Times,* Stanley Ellin, in the Sunday *New York Times Book Review,* was positively rapturous, calling it "vintage champagne." But its sales were not robust enough to make it Elman's breakout book that would take him from the limbo of the "midlist" to the empyrean of best sellers. I suspect that the publishers had something to do with this. Fred Jordan was hired at Methuen to terminate its American trade publishing activities (I know this because I, too, had a book on Methuen's list), and in its death throes, that house was less than robust in the way it promoted and sold books. Elman moved on to Macmillan with a Robert Harmon sequel set in his familiar Nicaragua, *The Menu Cypher,* but the jokes are less fresh, and the anger has made the humor even more bitter than in the first go-round. This anger was quite reasonable, because his experience with Methuen had not been good and his prospects with Macmillan were less than bright. That house was a Robert Maxwell operation that included the *New York Daily News* and the Berlitz schools, and the smarter editors were nervous although only the most prescient could have anticipated the collapse of the entire conglomerate and the suicide of its proprietor. In any event, like Methuen, and like Grosset and Dunlap, they were a bunch of bottom-feeders, looking to pick up on the cheap a good author whose career was on the decline but for whom there might yet be a temporary uptick from which they could take a short-term profit. And sooner or later, the author's self-deception frays and he figures out the unlovely terms of the relationship.

The ultimate adjustment, which is tough to make, isn't so much a matter of character as of the sheer need to write, no matter what. . . . Elman may have been done with the trade publishers of New York (or vice versa), but he was still working, still writing. There is *Disco Frito,* an appealing collection of short stories that Peregrine Smith published (they are a small press in Utah), and then *Tar Beach,* his best novel, which came out in 1991 from Sun & Moon Press (a small press in Los Angeles). But they are hard years of hand-to-mouth jobs at hostile or out-of-the-way places. He was at Penn from 1981 to 1982, then at Stony Brook in 1983, but that didn't work out so he was at the University of Arizona in 1985, at Michigan as the Hopwood visiting professor in 1988, and at Notre Dame in 1990.

Driven back, he starts again, from the beginnings we have already seen, but transformed now by a brilliant notion—the zany idea that the British had in response to the Kishinev pogroms when they offered Theodore Herzl a Jewish national homeland in Uganda. Elman imagines Peter Pintobasco, a young boy, hurt emotionally and physically too, who hangs out and daydreams on the Brooklyn synagogue roof where the community sunbathes—"Tar Beach"—putting them into a fantasy Africa where they speak "Swiddish" (a combination of Swahili and Yiddish), and where his father is Umpapa, a presence not quite so malign, perhaps, as Idi Amin, but not a nice guy, either. Very early on, Peter reveals himself a familiar Elman alter ego, when he is wondering about Crazy Mickey Rivlin who came back hurt from the war, having taken a piece of Japanese shrapnel in his head and who has tried to commit suicide, jumping off that roof. "Does it still hurt? Peter wonders, and touches the hot intact skull above his right ear near the temple, and the tiny stitches where Umpapa got mad at his report card with the 'D in deportment' and shoved him back against the radiator from pillar to post. That felt cold at first and then it hurt real bad, with lotsa blood, and he had to wear a white bandage around his head a whole week like a mummy."

The metaphors are complicated but they work without requiring any explanation. It is clear that, for all their pretensions to civility and culture, the adults are savages, are truly Ugandan, which the strange slippage of the Swiddish dialect underscores. At one point, "Peter squats, drawing with his spitty finger on the bricks," and there is a confrontation between him and his mother:

> Lillian arises, hitches up her bra, and across the hotness waddles over to her son, as though wading through a river of her own exuded grease.

Great block letters scrawl and spread, connected by loops of drying spittle, and sweat. There are whole areas already beginning to fade, though others seem unearthed with streaks of tar, like an ancient text from the windy grit of Tar Beach. What holy terror is this?

SCUM BAGS
BIG FAT COCKSUCKERS
FUCKING ADULT CHEAPSKATE NAZIS
OHURU!

(One might observe that *ohuru* is a combination of *uhuru*, the Swahili word for "freedom" that Robert Ruark's novel bearing that word as its title had popularized, and *kineahora*, which is a common pronunciation of the Yiddish expression that correctly is *kayn aynhoreh*, a magical phrase uttered to ward off the evil eye.)

Her hands spring out before she even thinks I will beat this child, my son, and she feels the flesh of his face and then his warm shoulder blades sting against her palms . . .

"You little monster. . . ." Wam. "Holy terror. . . ." She can't believe her own rage. "Juvenile Delinquent!"

"Mommy," he's shouting back. "Mommy!"

Her hands are wet with tears and sweat.

She slaps at him again. "To call your own mother such things . . . Calling me filth . . ."

"They're just words mommy please just words . . ."

Along with the Oedipal drama Freud describes, there is another fantasy children have, almost as common—that they are foundlings, that they have other parents somewhere, that their situation in this household with this mother and father has been the result of some terrible administrative error of the inattentive gods and that, somehow, it might one day be righted so that all will be well. With great tact and delicacy, and with robust wit, Elman plays on these dreams and the wonderful liveliness of children who contrive by these desperate measures somehow to survive to adulthood. Peter constructs an alternate universe out of tags of radio commercials, comic books, popular fiction, and, of course, the Yiddish that swirls around him, which, in our generation, our parents used as a secret language when they didn't want the children to understand what they were saying.

The subject of the novel is, really, Peter's progress toward understanding, seeing his parents and seeing through them. And its ways and means are those mostly of Joyce—*Portrait of the Artist as a Young Man* but translated to Brooklyn. It takes the donnée of *Fredi & Shirl & the Kids* but the anger of that book is now tempered by a sadness generous enough to extend to the little boy's oppressors. The earlier book, because of its limitations—not only of point of view but of vision—is essentially a récit; *Tar Beach* is a roman. The greater dimension of the achievement is not merely artistic but psychological and, finally, moral.

In my view, *Tar Beach* is a great book. It ought to have earned Elman a secure place among the first rank of American writers. What happened, of course, was considerably less than that—a favorable but uncomprehending one-paragraph notice on the "In Brief" page of the *New York Times Book Review* that called it "an elegant slice of life." (To be fair, they did put it on their list in December of the best novels of the year.) It was his last published novel, although there are at least two completed manuscripts that he left, one of which, *Love Handles,* is supposed to come out from Sun & Moon within the next year or so. *Cocktails at Somoza's* is also a great book but is out of print. Elman's last collection of poetry, *Cathedral-Tree-Train and Other Poems,* is the third of his extraordinarily fine and, indeed, essential volumes. The title piece is a forty-four-page elegy for the California painter Keith Sanzenbach, and what I find most interesting about this poem is how he puts pieces of his mental yammer that are already familiar to us from other contexts and other books to new uses. The epigraph, for instance, is from Attila Joszef, a Hungarian poet (the University at Szeged is named after him) who killed himself in 1937, and it could apply to *Tar Beach* as easily as to this poem: "An adult is one who has no father and mother in his heart."

One way to consider this meditation on the costly turmoil and creative extravagance of the San Francisco scene in the sixties is that, like *Tar Beach,* it is a poem about growing up, culturally, emotionally, artistically, and spiritually. This is not an enterprise to which our

perennially youthful and optimistic country has given much attention, but it is a crucial and necessary subject, a requirement for our
survival. In a prodrome gesture before his eventual suicide, Sanzenbach threatens to kill himself and Elman describes the event thus:

> He makes a picture called *Cathedral-Tree-Train,* stands
> in the sunlight of the window pointing a revolver toward his
> brain.
>   I imagine his tears like little jewels on his cheeks.
>   "Don't, Keith," I shout from Palo Alto across Dumbar-
> ton Bridge to somewhere in Walnut Creek. "*Don't . . .*"
>   A few minutes later he calls back; "Don't despair use
> your head save your hair use Fitch shampoo . . ."
>   ("I was just asking permission," Keith said, "I'd never
> do anything like that without asking your permission.")

The lines from the singing commercial for Fitch shampoo appear at
a crucial moment in *Tar Beach,* when little Peter learns that "Uncle
Izzy" is, in fact, his biological father, and he tells his father that he
knows. A few pages later, he is singing that jingle in the shower and
talking Swiddish, and he refers, in his father's presence, to "Uncle
Izzy . . ."

> "Don't ever call him that! Never call him that to me again."
> And long after the little man has disappeared behind one of the
> rows of lockers, Peter continues to sing:
> "Don't despair
> use your head
> save your hair
> use Fitch shampoo . . ."

It has been set up so that in the payoff, here, the boy realizes that he
has blundered, that he ought to have used his head to save not only
his hair but his life, and that, in unpredictable moments, the banali-
ties of radio jingles can turn ugly and real, with that "despair" being
a peculiar but not irrelevant threat he realizes he has been living with
all along.

In larger ways, too, the life of Keith Sanzenbach must have seemed familiar to Elman. Section 10 begins:

> "Please do not be shocked by what may appear a lack of emotional involvement," he wrote to me in the Army, at Fort Chaffee, Arkansas, when his wife left him for another man.
>
> Frequently,
> even before drugs tore him apart,
> shadows on Keith's face suggested he was numb,
> standing behind this rain
> of confusing, inappropriate responses:
> > "I am not without love for her."
> > "My main concern is her."
> > "I am not the sole factor of her development
> > but probably a hindrance . . ."
>
> Jealousy is sometimes very generous,
> and rage speaks in a sweet
> gentle voice.

The poem ventures into the borderlands between verse and prose, never quite relaxing into prosiness but willing to risk that in order to accommodate the messiness and sprawl that is the part of our experience that tight metrical organization cannot plausibly represent. Elman's poetry resembles, in this adventurousness, some of Mark Rudman's work, which I admire and from which I have learned a good deal. In his poetic practice, too, Elman's rebelliousness is apparent. He studied, after all, with Yvor Winters, in a graduate class in which Thom Gunn and Alan Stephens were his classmates. Winters, as Elman talks about him in *Namedropping*, was not an easy master to study under:

> The other day in the small north shore Long Island town where I live, I ran into a former member of Yvor Winters' Stanford poetry workshop. He is now a retired New York City high school teacher, this chunky, gentle, sad, slow-talking New York Jew who

has only just gotten back to writing poems again of some beauty and passion after his encounters with Winters in the workshop thirty-seven years ago.

Oddly, Winters invited this fellow to come all the way from Brooklyn College to Stanford on a full poetry fellowship and then proceeded to savage every poem he ever submitted to the workshop with arguments that ranged from close textual criticism to the ad hominem.

It was a brutal spectacle to watch this Coney Island Keatsian subjected to Winters' unrelenting persiflage. Even though Winters was as often accurate as not, Martin flayed was painful to observe.

Elman, however, would not be bullied. He persevered and refused to be either intimidated or co-opted. Winters recommended him for a Royal Victor graduate fellowship at Stanford, "which was a great honor and quite lucrative, though it meant I would have to take an ordinary Ph.D. in English literature," but Elman declined.

> I really didn't want to be one of Winters' epigones. I'd discovered prose and wanted to learn how to write it with vivid efficiency. This was probably a bad error of judgment on my part. If I'd stayed under Winters' protection I might have made a living at some college or university without all the dislocations and stresses I've undergone. But I was always too much frightened of Winters . . . I didn't think I'd be able to hold my head above the water.

(As I type this out, I notice that "epigones" is a word he used about Singer, too. And the coincidence suggests that Elman recognized that he had, with both men, gone through a similar process in which, as he searched for a suitable father figure, his hopes were briefly raised and then dashed.)

We have seen, in any event, enough of those safe university careers to know what they do to a writer and to understand, as I am sure Elman did, even as he wrote these words, that his instincts had been right. And in the end, he came back to poetry, for, as he observed in his autobiographical essay for *Contemporary Authors Autobiography Series* (Gale Research Co., Detroit, 1986), "I now believe I

am more of a poet than a prose writer, though I still make a living
writing novels and journalism. I love to write poems. I love language, and movement, and action, and despise carefulness that lacks
caring. I wish somebody would ask me to teach the stuff sometime."

Winters's tutelage, if it did not involve the use of Mr. Strap,
surely was surely harsh enough to remind Elman of Mr. Hitler the
Bully, incarnations of whom were all too frequent in his life. But for
those who survive a tyrannical father and don't break, there is a kind
of strength that can be invaluable later on. In his struggle with Winters, Elman knew that he'd won, or at least survived, and, as he says
in "A Letter to the Dead," a poem in *Cathedral-Tree-Train* addressed
to his former teacher:

> I believe then I knew I had to fight for my own life:
> Ten years later I heard you were dead
> of cancer of the tongue.

Elman's strength and wit and talent were his weapons against the
barbarities that beset him, not only from parents and teachers, from
whom he had the right to expect better, but also editors, reviewers,
and faculty colleagues. What he learned from that harshness was that
kindness and love, when one encounters them, are rare and all the
more precious. He had his family and his friends, who loved and
understood him.

I am proud that I was one of those friends.

So There Were
These Two Jews:
The Poetry of
Irving Feldman

IN AN EXTRAORDINARILY GRACEFUL ESSAY in *The Poetry of Irving Feldman: Nine Essays,* edited by Harold Schweitzer (Bucknell University Press, 1992), Denis Donoghue begins his observations almost apologetically: "I can't claim that his people are my people, his God my God; I can't speak of the Holocaust, I can't claim to stand within a particular representative privilege by the war, except in the sense which must be notional that we are all, whatever else we are, human. We have sympathies, correspondences, certain powers, however limited, of imaginative identification." And he goes on to claim a relation with the poetry that is, as he calls it, "provisional in perhaps limiting senses."

My own relationship to Irving Feldman's poems is different, closer but still with a reach. Feldman was born in 1928, so his experience of World War II was more vivid than mine. His bar mitzvah would have been in 1941, a hell of a year to come into moral responsibility. Mine, in 1948, was a couple of months before Israel's declaration of independence—a much more hopeful time. My mother was born in Brooklyn, where Feldman comes from, but she'd moved up, so that I am a native of Westchester County. Feldman went to City College ("Football, baseball, swimming in the tank! / We got money but we keep it in the bank"), while I was sent off to Andover and Yale ("Boolah, boolah!").

We both made our debuts as poets in 1961, when Atlantic/Little Brown published his *Works and Days* and Scribner's brought out my *Suits for the Dead* in their Poets of Today series. My copy of *Works and Days* has its dust jacket still intact, and that sports a blurb from John Crowe Ransom: "Irving Feldman is a very sound poet [whatever the hell that means: perhaps that he is not a loony like Lowell and Jarrell and some of the other students Ransom found clustering around him], and I would not care to limit the extent of his triumph when I think about his promise as a poet. [Again, this is gnomic at best, meaning that Feldman is not so dreadful that one can't imagine him going on to write something of value someday.] I should remark particularly upon the rapidity with which he develops his natural talent. [What other kind is there, sir?] He has great versatility, and a very obvious passion for the art."

But the blurb's words don't matter; it's the signature that counts. As probably the words of my first published poem don't matter so much as that they appeared in John Crowe Ransom's *Kenyon Review*. This makes us, in some vague way, kin. We were both bright kids, at any rate, and we have both grown up to be Jewish American poets. There are differences of course. He confronts the Shoah and I don't, or at least not directly. In some ways, I am afraid to do so. I also have reservations about my right to talk of such things. I wasn't there and for me, it is, just barely, history. I only heard about it later. On the other hand, I also have a sense that anything one talks about now is in the light (or darkness) of that, so one needn't address that subject directly. It is in the air we breathe, a faint sickening odor of burning flesh. (The title poem of my collection, *Crossroads*, alludes to the destruction of the Jews in Poland, but only to say that we missed that. Our family came here to a better life—and it was here that my mother was bludgeoned to death by a burglar and died unhistorically and alone. And I do recognize that in extremis, in times of the most profound grief and despair, the Holocaust is what comes to mind as the gold standard of suffering and evil.)

Feldman's "Pripet Marshes" and "To the Six Million" are among his best known poems, and I admire them. But I am, in various ways and to differing degrees, uncomfortable about them—but not in the way that I am sometimes uncomfortable with the writings of Primo Levi or in the company of friends who were in the camps and have numbers tattooed on their arms. "The Pripet Marshes," the more successful of these, is probably one of the dozen or so most interesting and powerful poems of our generation. It is a marvel of strategic manipulation, disarming almost any objection any reader can bring to it—moral, aesthetic, or anywhere in between. It begins:

> Often I think of my Jewish friends and seize them as they are
>   and transport them in my mind to the *shtetlach* and ghettos,
>
> And set them walking the streets, visiting, praying in *shul*,
>   feasting and dancing. The men I set to arguing, because I
>   love dialectic and song—my ears tingle when I hear their
>   voices—and the girls and women I set to promenading or to
>   cooking in the kitchens, for the sake of their tiny feet and
>   clever hands.

They are not real people, but constructions of the poet, transpositions of his friends in Brooklyn whom he *imagines* there, as he is free to do. The poem is not about them, then, but him. He toys with the thought of the arriving Germans:

> But there isn't a second to lose, I snatch them all back.
> For when I want to, I can be a God.
> No, the Germans won't have one of them:
> This is my people, they are mine!
>
> And I flee with them, crowd out with them: I hide myself in a
>   pillowcase
> stuffed with clothing, in a woman's knotted
>   handkerchief, in a shoebox.

And one by one I cover them in mist, I take them out.
The German motorcycles zoom through the town,
They break their fists on the hollow doors.
But I can't hold out any longer. My mind clouds over.
I sink down as though drugged or beaten.

He admits, in other words, that this is a self-indulgence, the playact-
ing of an imaginative and terrified young man, and he acknowledges
the temptation, or the compulsion, to daydream in this way. But the
defeat of it is real and is a tiny morsel, perhaps, of the historical catastrophe. And after he has made such a strategic rhetorical admission, which of us can think of denying his modest claim or charging
him with bad faith?

In his new book, *The Life and Letters*, the opening poem, "The
Dream," demonstrates a similar dramatic virtuosity. Here Feldman
offers a series of "takes" and "toppers" that are closer to a Lenny
Bruce routine than they are to the work of the major British and
American poets we both studied in school. He begins:

Once, years after your death, I dreamt
you were alive and that I'd found you
living once more in the old apartment.
But I had taken a woman up there
to make love to in the empty rooms.
I was angry at you who'd borne and loved me
and because of whom I believed in heaven.
I regretted your return from the dead
and said to myself almost bitterly,
"For godsakes, what was the big rush,
couldn't she wait one more day?"

The tone is comic, as the diction ("For godsakes") and syntax of the
direct quote make clear. The situation is comic, too, a sitcom awkwardness that Feldman also suggests with the flatfootedness, even the
ungainliness of the piece. "But I had taken a woman up there / to
make love to in the empty rooms" is an aggressive display of prepo-
sitions that is deliberately unpoetic.

Then we get the turn, the topper:

> And just so daily somewhere Messiah
> is shunned like a beggar at the door because
> someone has something he wants to finish
> or just something better to do, something
> he prefers not to put off forever
> —some little pleasure so deeply wished
> that Heaven's coming has to seem bad luck
> or worse, God's intruding selfishness!

Okay, fine, wonderful, because as Platonists have always recognized, the trick is getting the big ideas to connect to the real world, the one we live in. And the move he has made has managed to do that, in a startling and satisfactory way. But then there's a topper on the topper, the further peripeteia he's been aiming at all along:

> But you always turned Messiah away
> with a penny and a cake for his trouble
> —because wash had to be done, because
> who could let dinner boil over and burn,
> because everything had to be festive for
> your husband, your daughters, your son.

A lovely piece of business, really. Having swapped the grumpy and disgraceful guy whose mother's ghost has shown up at the wrong moment for the mother herself upon whom Messiah had come to call, he has also changed the motives for the turning away of heaven from his lust and self-absorption to her duty and love. Now he can feel guilt both ways, toward Messiah and toward his mother, too, because when she turned God away it was for wholly admirable and lovable reasons. Indeed, it was for him. The fact that this is a dream also means that we can't really criticize it as just another piece of Jewish self-hatred. Dreams, we have been forced to understand, have a truth in them and a privilege, too, because the dreamer isn't responsible for his choice of subject. All we can do is look at the craftsmanship of the literary presentation and admire its inexorability, especially in that last couple of lines where the beneficiaries of the mother's altruism are listed in ascending order . . . "your husband, your daughters, your son."

I am always interested in excellent work. But what fascinates me about this particular piece in this new book is how this is altogether different in kind from what Chaucer, Spenser, Donne, Milton, Dryden, Pope, Wordsworth, and Eliot taught us how to do and validated as legitimate tactics and strategies for poetry in English. This is structurally closer to Jewish *shpritzing*. Consider an old bare-bones Joan Rivers joke. She tells her husband that (a) he's got to stop coming to dinner in his undershirt, and then, after a breath, adds the topper, (b) that he should "at least put on his underpants," and then gives us the topper on that, (c) "if not for my sake, then for your mother's." This gets a laugh, which she trumps with (d) "Or we'll never be allowed into this restaurant again." That such homey and homely devices can enable poems of dramatic monologue as engaging as anything in Browning or Cavafy is delightful. And it seems to me a sign of Feldman's development over the years as he has grown more and more confident of his gifts and tastes.

The other well-known poem I mentioned earlier, one that I confess I don't like so much, is "For the Six Million," and what I find uncomfortable about it is that it sounds too much like T. S. Eliot. As Christopher Ricks and Anthony Julius have amply demonstrated, this is a particularly unfortunate resonance for such a subject, but the resonance is, I think, unmistakable:

> If there is a god,
> he descends from the power.
> But who is the god rising from death?
> (So, thunder invades the room, and brings with it
> a treble, chilly and intimate, of panes rattling
> on a cloudy day in winter.
> But when I look through the window,
> a sudden blaze of sun is in the streets,
> which are, however, empty and still. The thunder
> repeats.) Thunder here. The emptiness resounds
> here on the gods' struggle ground

> where the infinite negative retreats,
> annihilating where it runs,
> and the god who must possess pursues, pressing
> on the window panes, passing through.

The metrics, the occasional rhymes, the images, the mood and diction are a reasonably deft mélange of Eliotic lines. That "thunder" and the rhyme of "retreats" and "streets" make it especially hard to ignore. But the posture troubles me too, striking me as artsy and pompous and fundamentally wrong. It is as if Feldman had despaired of all the intricacy of "The Pripet Marshes"—the poem that immediately precedes this one in *New and Selected Poems*—and he wanted to tell us, "Hey, listen here, the Holocaust was . . . serious stuff!" To this suggestion we are likely to feel some resistance, not because we disagree but because we'd already managed to figure that out for ourselves.

I mention this poem not to belittle Feldman's accomplishments but rather to suggest something about the course of his development over the years. This and "The Pripet Marshes" appeared more than thirty years ago, after all. Now, in *The Life and Letters* he gives us another piece on the same subject, or at least a related subject, "Outrage Is Anointed by Levity, or Two Laureates A-Lunching." The poem carries an epigraph from Joseph Brodsky's 1987 Nobel lecture:

> "How can one write poetry after Auschwitz?"
> inquired Adorno . . . "And how can one eat lunch?"
> the American poet Mark Strand once retorted. In any
> case, the generation to which I belong has proven capable
> of writing that poetry.

This time, there is no possum posturing but a clearly established *shpritzing* persona, a street-smart, smart-assed guy refusing to be taken in by those literary types. He begins:

> *In any case* (or, as our comedians say,
> "But seriously folks"), has Adorno's question
> been disposed of, interred beneath the poems

> written since Auschwitz?—rather than raised again
> and again like a ghost by each of them?

> In any case, one would like very much to know
> how one *can* eat one's lunch after Auschwitz.
> Can you tell me that, please?

The allusion to comedians' routines is not only startling but curiously necessary and right. Comics, after all, are the people who speak about the unspeakable. That's their job. Indeed, one could make a case that the mission of the Jews in the past couple of centuries has been to speak about the unspeakable, Marx and Freud having brought the previously taboo subjects of money and sex into our public fora and private salons. It is for this reason, perhaps, that so many of our great clowns have been Jews, from Jack Benny, Milton Berle, and Henny Youngman through Lenny Bruce and Mort Sahl and up to Roseanne, Richard Lewis, and (God help us) Howard Stern. Comedy is to the Jews what the blues are to African Americans. So if there is to be an answer to Adorno's question, or to Strand's probably more intelligent question, then it is likely have a vaudeville brashness to it. It may be that the brashness is, itself, at least part of the answer.

> NOT, let it be said, *fearfully*
> Certainly NOT *despairingly*
> Therefore NOT *painfully*
> NOT forgodsakes *starvingly*
> NOT *weepingly*
> NOT *resignedly*
> NOT, please, *horribly, hideously, moribundly!*

> HOWEVER, should one, *bizarrely,* encounter
> difficulty in eating lunch after Auschwitz
> one can do it in the following manner:

The capitalization and italics sprinkled so aggressively into this tzimmes may require some comment. It is impossible to read these lines without taking exaggerated postures that are campy and self-mocking and that therefore put the assertions the text is making at some remove from the writer. If these are stage directions, the inevitable implication is that a performance is going on.

Actually, there is the further implication that Adorno, Strand, and even Brodsky are performing, too. And there is conceivably an additional suggestion that none of this may be in what Miss Manners would call good taste. All these notes continue to sound, indeed to blare forth as from a choir of sackbuts:

> First of all, HEARTILY and CHUCKLINGLY, as an example of
> good health, infectious optimism, faith in humanity.
> Then LOVINGLY, SAVORINGLY, to show one is lovable, always a delight to observe.
> And CHARMINGLY, assuring one's food of one's civil intentions.
> Then it will *wish* to be consumed by one.
> And CONVIVIALLY, since company always adds zest, even to a
> menu of sawdust.

These adverbs in caps don't just risk ugliness but court it, insist on it—chucklingly. And the periphrases, as in "Then it will *wish* to be consumed by one," are a kind of defiance of pompous bureaucratic and academic discourse. These categories are beggared by the subject, rendered pitiably irrelevant and effete. Feldman (or the persona of the speaker, anyway) is frantic, shameless, and urgent:

> But also LANGUIDLY and as if POORMOUTHINGLY, not to
> attract the attentions of the envious or the merely hungry.
> Yet INNOCENTLY, because like, man, I didn't do it—I mean, I
> wasn't even there!
> Which is to say, FEELINGFULLY, because one *has* feelings—
> doesn't *everyone?*
> And so RETORTINGLY, even QUIPPINGLY, and (seriously
> folks)
> RIGHTEOUSLY, since poets *must* keep up their strength
> if they are to prove capable of writing poems "after Auschwitz,"
> being mindful of the mindlessness everywhere about them, for it
> is their singular task to promulgate the

deepest human agendas.
And therefore, GENEROUSLY, since one is eating (whether *they*
    know it or not) for others, for civilization itself.
One is (to put it in a nutshell) *lunching for Auschwitz*.

It works itself up almost to dementia, which is not at all inappropriate. Who are these pompous bozos anyway, these *Aufklarung* mavens,
these Nobel laureates or poets laureate, to presume to be "promul-
gating the deepest human agendas"? They are poseurs, potzers,
putzes! And if they can't say anything appropriate and proportion-
ate, they should shut up.

It is, up to this point, a great bravura performance, quite different
from "The Pripet Marshes" and even bolder. Surely, it is every bit as
fine. Feldman doesn't trust it, however, or doesn't trust it enough. He
goes on with two more sections, and as any borscht-belt tummler
ought to know, you should never follow a comic with another who is
less funny.

Feldman has made his point, but he wants to make sure we "get
it." So he gives us these eight lines:

> "And how can one eat lunch" after Auschwitz?
> High, high is the noble dais where godlings sup
> and from hog heaven splat down their pearls on us.
> So outrage is anointed by levity.
> So levity is solemnized for the world.
>
> And all we shall know of apocalypse
> is not the shattering that follows but
> brittleness before, the high mindlessness, the quips.

This isn't the poem anymore but an explication of the poem incor-
porated into the text. Feldman is brooding here about the implication
of the speaker and of the reader, pointing out, as if it were necessary
to make it any more explicit, that this is not really a proper subject for
levity. It is not a good sign that this kind of joking, Strand's or his
own, is permissible. The "high mindlessness, the quips" may be, perhaps a sinister prodrome. But the brighter readers have already fig-

ured this out, I'd expect. (And to the slower ones there is no point in talking.)

There is then a third section I don't have the heart to type out in extenso and like less even than the second, a breathy and stagy performance that ends:

> this poem
> asks
> how could you
> how can you
> silence asks
> this poem
> unable to answer
> silence
> unable
> and yet writes
> the silence
> out

But if I hate that, I can ignore it. And even hating it, I can see how it is different from "For the Six Million," or at least not derivative in quite the same way. What troubles me is that it is redolent of a kind of 1930s artiness. It certainly doesn't have the astonishing brashness of the first section of the poem that asserts life (or at least lunch) and also declares to us that such assertions, however graceless, however brutal and tasteless, are the only "answer" to Auschwitz.

But the faults of a poet are, in a blessed way, irrelevant. There can be a hundred flawed poems, but if there is one that is good enough— and lucky enough—to strike the right note or appear in the right anthology, that single piece can earn its author a small immortality. Think of Henry King's "Exequy." (And now think of *another* poem by Henry King!)

Poets, Auden remarks somewhere, are not necessarily the best judges of the work of their fellow practitioners. They ignore what is excellent and look for what is congenial, or, more candidly, what they can adopt, adapt, or steal from. The congeniality of a poet is not something that professors of English are comfortable talking about, but it is true that one has one's favorite poets—as Picasso suggested—in the way one has one's favorite pipe tobacco, wine, cheese, or breed of dog. To put the contrary case, a reader who responds to all poetry with the same degree of interest and enthusiasm probably doesn't have a lot of enthusiasm.

This is all a cumbersome way of suggesting that Feldman's work speaks to me with an intimacy and that I respond to it with parts of myself that few poets call into play. And one of his pieces I find myself returning to with the highest expectations that it never fails to satisfy is his odd meditation on "The Little Children of Hamelin," in which he takes the Robert Browning poem and turns it from a caprice to a dirge.

The gesture of the turning, first, demands a brief observation. I like smart-assedness. I approve entirely of George Starbuck's debonair "To His Chi. Mistress," or Anthony Hecht's truly brilliant "The Dover Bitch." But they are taking serious poems and making fun of them. To take something that was fun to start with and turn it into deadly earnest is a kind of gesture I associate with Shostakovich, where the William Tell (or Lone Ranger) theme of Rossini turns into something heartbreaking and cosmic in the Fifteenth Symphony, where, among other things, the dying composer is bidding goodbye to each of the instrument groups.

Feldman takes the piece Browning wrote to amuse an invalid child, an exercise in comic doggerel, and transforms it into a rumination on holocausts, because that, after all, was what was happening in Hamelin in 1376. Whether or not it is because the mayor and the council were deadbeats and had failed to pay the exterminator's bill, the piper leads all the children to Koppelberg Hill, where they disappear through "a wondrous portal," into a world that the lone lame survivor describes as:

> a joyous land
> Joining the town and just at hand,
> Where waters gushed and fruit-trees grew
> And flowers put forth a fairer hue,
> And everything was strange and new;
> The sparrows were brighter than peacocks here,

And their dogs outran our fallow deer,
And honey-bees had lost their stings,
And horses were born with eagles' wings . . .

Well, that's all very nice if we can believe it. Feldman sees it another way, and thinks, perhaps, of the bizarre business of those string quartets that played to welcome the victims to the Nazi death camps. That grimness, at any rate, is what he sees in the story that Browning used to so drastically different an effect:

Suddenly the pipe was still, piper was gone.
In the place of his mouth a river squirmed, squealed
—one endless rat of one million rats drowning
and drowned: Rat River, cobbled with sleek rat backs
and wet rat bellies, where little rat feet slipped
and caught in the thatch of rat whiskers and tails.
Black bubbles boiled up gleaming and looked at us.
White foam raged and gnawed at the night for breath.
Abandoned by music, and frightened to death
by death, then and there we'd have turned and run home,
but the wind at our backs brought us happy sounds
of children who scraped our bowls and rolled our hoops
and called our pets—laughing, golden children, grown
from gold coins our parents hoarded when we left.

"You can, you can, come over here, come over here,
if you are light enough, slight enough, faint enough . . ."
little voices were calling out, and calling out
from over the squealing river, "I'm lonely here!"
—runaway children, abandoned and lost children,
stolen children, and strays, and foundlings, and poor waifs
sold to be someone's slaves were calling out to us;
and the ghost children we children would never have
from the distant shore were singing, "Please play with me!"
But when we crossed to them, we found no place at all,
no children there, but voices saying, voices singing,

> "You can, you can, be music too, be music too,
> forever, and forevermore." And so, and so, we were.

It is an elegant thing to echo, by the repetitions, of the last couple of lines in particular, the tinkling of the Browning, but modulated to the sonorities of grief. It would have been possible to end there, but Feldman goes on, but not losing his concentration and focus. Rather, he rings one further change, addressing the reader in the voice of the lost children:

> *If on a summer's night, unable to sleep,*
> *you throw open the window to a starry sky,*
> *and the softest air from far off enters your head,*
> *and life is wide with possibility again,*
> *before returning to the sweetness of your bed*
> *and the charmed oblivion of your dreaming,*
> *remember us lost on night's farthest shore,*
> *and linger on a little while at your window*
> *to hum, though faint and broken, this story you hear.*
> *Buy yourself back, father, mother, you can,*
> *you can, for the price of a song, you can,*
> *from death—and take us in, feel us, feel*
> *us, give us a home here in your breath!*

The syntactical ambiguity is intricate and elegant, a nudging, I think, toward the trance state to which Feldman is leading us. Much of the craft of poetry turns out to be the rhetorical equivalent of the techniques of hypnotic induction. One of those techniques involves a kind of confusion, so that the subject seizes with all the greater fervor on whatever line of clear meaning may present itself to the flustered consciousness. One can read the "father, mother," either as objects of "Buy" or as vocatives, but either way, or both ways, there can be a restoration, and "for the price of a song"—which is, at the same time nearly nothing or a princely richness—a reparation and a healing can at least to some degree be achieved.

And do we believe that? Perhaps, because Feldman's poem has

admitted so much more than Browning's, we may be willing to risk such a leap of faith. Or we may be forced, by our recognition that the alternative is despair, to take that leap whether we expect to succeed or not.

The Poetry
of Grief

IN THE PRESENCE OF PAIN, which they see as a professional challenge, the reaction of physicians, social workers, psychologists, and grief counselors is to want to alleviate it. Grief and depression are kinds of pain, and, for them, any pain is an invitation to intervene and do good. Given such a set of predispositions, and given, also, the optimism of American culture, it is not surprising that grief, as these experts talk about it, should turn into "the grief process," a locution that somehow suggests that there is a natural history through which one ought to progress as efficiently as possible to a healthy "resolution." This template, which is less restrictive than it used to be, derives from suggestions in Freud's discussion of "normative" and "melancholic" mourning, which, like much else in Freud's work, was schematized and to some extent vulgarized as it trickled down into the culture of medicine.

Until recently, grief counselors used to label those who didn't respond to their ministrations in a timely fashion as dysfunctional.

They did not go so far as actually to accuse such people of ingrati-
tude, but they assigned them to a special category called "complicated grief."

But it wasn't—and it isn't—at all complicated. On the contrary,
it is simple and overwhelming. Inconsolable grief is not so much a
disability or a disease, or even a condition, as it is a new identity. Literally. They recognized the truth of this transformation in imperial
China, my daughter informs me, by adding a suffix to the name of a
person in mourning. For a year, the merchant and butcher and draper
would address someone who had experienced a loss as "Mr. Bereaved
Person," and, for someone who had lost a parent or a child, it was
two years.

Our modern medical, social, and psychological vocabularies are
not well equipped to handle metaphysical and spiritual questions, but
it can happen that in one's grief and despair, the world reveals itself
in a new aspect, allowing a darker view of the truth of the human
condition than one may perhaps have acknowledged—or did acknowledge but could not, until the moment of catastrophe, truly
comprehend. This is what I take Aeschylus to mean when he says in
the *Agamemnon* that "wisdom comes from suffering."

At the furthest end of the spectrum—for those, say, who have
undergone torture or have been in concentration camps—that experience continues forever as the norm from which any variation is
only an unreliable respite. One can describe this alteration of attitude
as pathology, or, having no particular warrant to question its legiti-
macy, one can at least speculate about whether Aeschylus may have
been right. In a culture that has been not only secularized but trivial-
ized, wisdom, in any event, is in short supply. What one discovers in
agony may not be the only truth, but is nonetheless *a* truth. What
physicians and therapists may be finding in the afflicted people they
are trying to treat is that this is not merely an alteration in the limbic
system but a new, intimate, and unintellectual relationship to the
tragedy of the human condition. And wisdom so expensively ac-
quired is not something one is willing to relinquish.

Let me cite a few lines from the end of Stephen Dunn's "The
Vanishings," from his *New and Selected Poems 1974–1994:*

You understand and therefore hate
because you hate the passivity of understanding
that your worst rage and finest
private gesture will flatten and collapse
into history, become invisible
like defeats inside houses. Then something happens
(it is happening) which won't vanish fast enough,
your voice fails, chokes to silence;
hurt (how could you have forgotten?) hurts.
Every other truth in the world, out of respect,
slides over, makes room for its superior.

Hurt, as he says and as everyone knows, hurts. But it is the possibility of that "superiority" that I want particularly to emphasize. I don't at all mean to suggest that the doctors and social workers shouldn't continue to offer what help they can give to those who want it. But I do want to raise the possibility that not everyone wants it, and that there may be reasons for the reluctance of some sufferers to let go of their pain.

Poetry, as Auden tells us, makes nothing happen, but it can offer insights into what is going on. In Jahan Ramazani's recent book, *Poetry of Mourning*,[1] there is an interesting observation about how the modern elegy has become, almost, antielegy, a reaction to the pieties of "Lycidas" and "In Memoriam." The modern elegy, Ramazani suggests, is "a compromise-formation in its response to the privatization of grief; yet as published discourse, it carries out in the public realm its struggle against the denial of grief. Moreover, the modern elegy enables the work of mourning in the face of social suppression, but it also instances that suppression, often displacing and mocking grief."

What one might add to that is the more general observation about the overarching mystery of poetry, which is that a poet can write something quite private and readers can respond to it, supplying from their own lives those energizing details that the literary work

1. University of Chicago Press, 1994.

invites and exploits. A recent sonnet of mine explores how this may
happen:

INK

Poised above the paper, the pen's nib
is gravid with ink, a tremulous black droplet
by which one can learn to calibrate fluctuations
of weather, inner and outer, as if it were crimson
liquid that lives in thermometers' wells: a poet's
day is not merely his own, for clouds as they drift
across his skies will darken or brighten your own.
Or is it yet stranger? When San Gennaro's dried

blood liquefies in the phial, the people of Naples
offer up prayers of thanks, but the miracle's true
work is within their own hearts where freshets of faith,
of hope, and even of charity run renewed.
His drop of ink can do that too: it dries
but later flows elsewhere in your tears, your blood.

Eliot says somewhere that in bad poetry, those things that ought
to be conscious are left unconscious, and those things that ought to
be left unconscious are made conscious. Another way of describing
this mysterious business is to think of a poem as an act of discovery.
(Frost used to say, "No surprise for the writer; no surprise for the
reader.") If the poet knows what he is going to discover, the poem is
probably not worth writing. What I did not realize during the writing of the foregoing was its connection with an earlier poem about
my mother's murder, in 1982:

BLOODY MURDER

Beauty and truth may dally together,
but when it comes time to pop the question,
it's ugliness that settles in
to take the vows with truth for the long
haul, the enduring and faithful companion.
The difficult lesson we must all study

is how to be children of such a marriage
and honor what we cannot love.

After the burglar bludgeoned my mother
to death with a bathroom scale and a large
bottle of Listerine, the police
recommended Ronny Reliable's
Cleaning Service—one of a growing
number of firms that make it their business
to clean up after messy murders,
suicides, and other disasters.

They have the solvents and strong stomachs
for such work. I still wonder
who would choose that kind of employment
or what the men who performed this awful
and intimate task looked like. We only
spoke on the phone; detectives let them
in; and the charge showed up on my next
Mastercard bill. But I know they were there.

The chemical smell hung in the air
of the empty house for nearly a month,
proving they'd been there and done the job,
which is to say that the other unthinkable
thing had happened first. Excess,
whether of pleasure or pain beggars
belief so that lovers and mourners rub
their eyes in similar ways, trying
to take in the thought along with the image.

One needs both. On the KLH
radio my mother kept on
top of the bureau there was a white
electric cord the assiduous workers
missed with its evidence a doubting
Thomas needs or dares, to challenge
nerve and love, the reliquary
stain of what had been done and undone.

It wasn't a bouillon cube, would not
reconstitute in heat and water,
but there it was, to be faced, the mark
of faceless functionaries, furies,
or Ronny Reliable's Cleaning Service.
Jesus knew how it was—and wasn't—
a comfort to tell his stunned disciples:
this is my body, this is my blood.

The blood at the end of "Ink," then, is not mere blood, but relates to that of my mother and, through her, that of Jesus.

The course of grief and recovery from "normal" losses is quite different, and I wrote a poem about my mourning for my father called "Solstice" because that's when he died and one learns how these things are marked in the cycle of the year.

SOLSTICE

A ghost of a sun flees from the sky as I,
the son of a ghostly father, hurry—to keep
blood circulating in the cold—to buy
another Yahrzeit candle in its cheap
glass I'll use for juice. I don't believe
in any of this, but he did, and I'd rather
feel like a fool than a bum. To think, to grieve,
to remember isn't enough. One must go to the bother
of doing something. Parents and children trade
places after awhile. I learned to endure
the whims, and accommodate to demands he made,
as he had done for mine once. Fewer and fewer
remain except for this minimal annual task.
A postcard comes from the people who did the stone
that marks the grave, so I don't have to ask
what date the Hebrew lunacy falls on.
They put it to me: will I refuse to do
what I know he would have wanted? I give in,
go out, come back again, still wanting to

earn praise as the good boy I've never been.
And when the sun has given up, I give
lip service, mumble the prayer, and light the wick.
It's guaranteed that the little flame will live
the whole twenty-four hours, which seems a trick
for two and three-quarter ounces of paraffin.
All night shadows will dance on the ceiling and play
on the walls. And as I pass, I will glance in
to see how it's doing during the next day.
The flame is life, but the candle's guttering is
a reenacting of the death. I take
small satisfaction in my bearing this
as well as I do. I know it's for my sake
as much as his that I do this. My eyes brim,
but that can happen at the movies. Say
rather that I've bargained once more with him
and done what he wanted, only to keep him at bay.

The companion poem to this is "Equinox," which demonstrates the difference between that "normal" grief I felt for my father's death and what my sister and I felt—and still feel—about the murder of our mother:

EQUINOX

1

A balance shifts, and we can feel the night
heavy in the scale; darkness and cold
will weigh with us from now on. In decline
the sun will make its doddering round of days
that are less than days, the ghosts of days, the weather
will turn, and the year, stricken, will sicken into
death.
            It is all just as it ought to be.
This is the day when we call one another
to exchange whatever comfort we can. This is
the day mother was murdered. And the sun

ought to blanch, to blench in shame. For all
our days are ghosts. This is our time of year.

    2

In Yiddish, *Yahrzeit*. There is no English word
that serves correctly. *Anniversary*
is gay, wears party hats, has dinner out,
but *Yahrzeit* tells the time by throbs of pain,
mourns the turning of each season's screws,
and can predict by inner aches the outer
weather,
               as the wounded learn to do
from predictable cycles of agony and numbness.
Pain and its diminution are the two
companions we trust, stars in our firmament.
We also have the telephone and each other.

    3

The world being what it is, it has a term
describing us. The social scientists call
us "catastrophic orphans," and study us
along with survivors of floods and such disasters,
and also torture victims. One theory holds
that the chemistry of the brain undergoes some changes
so that everything else changes
                        for them, for us.
It's plausible perhaps. At least we know
that what we know, we know. The others are lucky
and, whatever their ages, innocent as children.
We talk sometimes as children, but hurt children.

    4

One would suppose the past to be secure,
but no, its memories, even locked away,
are vulnerable to any passing thug

or crazy who can crawl through a cellar window
to wreak his retroactive havoc on any
treasure he fouls. The house, and the sense we had
of place that an alewife has or a spawning salmon
can find in its right river and freshwater pond
of welcome and safety is lost,

                                    burgled, robbed.
Sickened, we swim through indifferent seas, all
salty, none worth notice. I would not,
hating that place, go back, even to die.

    5

Whatever people live for, happy times,
the milestones of graduations, weddings, births,
occasions of reunion and rejoicing,
these are tainted. Now, no good news comes
but with its confirming pang

                                    that she has not
heard it, shared it, lived to see what she
would have blessed. And that lack of her blessing is
accursed. No child of ours achieves, enjoys
good fortune but to start our scalding tears.
Dutiful children, we rub our eyes with our fists
as she would have us do, we are sure, having
learned from her what good manners demand.

    6

It doesn't get better. Years have gone by
and the only change is that we no longer expect
or fear that we may somehow regain our old
lives and selves. We are like the religious
brothers and sisters of some strict observance,
except that we do not pray, unless to bear
witness is a kind of prayer.

                                    I doubt it.

What kind of play is it when Orestes
only shakes his head when Electra calls
to complain or, worse, not to complain but like
a good sister cheer him a little, to help him
bear it, bear up, get through another week?

7

The earth itself is the great mother, Gaea.
The Judeo-Christian view, always upward,
ignores such perceptions, primitive, basic,
as are under their very noses. The ground we walk
no longer springs, for the converse is also true,
that Mother was the earth. Her murder pollutes
like a chemical seepage or oil spill, and the fish
die and the birds and animals drop. On the news,
the clips are horrible, horrible.
                                        You and I,
stricken, can take grim satisfaction in these
dreadful confirmations that our worst
truth is not the exception, but that our
suffering has its company, is the rule.

8

We keep a few relics. I take care
of a pot of her African violets. Still alive,
they bloom in the spring and make me weep. But we,
being parts of her, are each other's keepsakes,
what's best of what is left of her, which changes
all the rules, for we must be good children,
tender with one another as if she had only
left the room a moment and would be back
to call us to account.
                            She is not watching
which puts us on our honor. What's hard to learn
is to forgive each other, as she would have done,
and harder, hardest, to forgive ourselves.

9

All day I have been playing Pergolesi's
Stabat Mater, the melancholy of it
bearably remote, dog-Latin, Catholic.
And yet, the two voices, the boy soprano
and countertenor are close enough,

                                  ours,
echoing, harmonizing and descanting,
as we do. *"Eja, Mater, fons amoris . . ."*
and I can scarcely breathe, for the gentleness
that cradled us from a brute and ugly world
is gone, and we are bereft. But like those two,
in harmony. A solo voice would be
intolerable. At least we are together.

10

The other blessing is that the cold will come.
The season is turning, has turned, and the first
frost will come with its usual relief,
killing by hundreds of millions, flies, mosquitoes,
midges, and other such creatures that teemed and annoyed
for what seemed at the time a long time. The stars
will twinkle again in icy-clear air with a hint
of anaesthesia if not peace, those scary
spaces in between impressive . . .
                              We don't
believe in souls up there spinning around
forever like Laika, but emptiness, cold
and darkness are good enough. I'd call that heaven.

What I have been trying to demonstrate may seem more like hurt
than wisdom. But there is wisdom that comes from the tragic view of
life, or, if you will, from grief and even depression. We ought not
look to literature for specific answers, but there can be solace and encouragement in the suffering of others, or in our observation of how

they bore it. Among the most sublime moments of drama, after all,
are the deaths of Lear and of Oedipus. My own tribulation has made
me, very probably, a better poet and a better reader. I understand
some things more deeply. This is a relatively recent poem I wrote
about Rabbi Nachman of Bratslav, one of the great Hasidic masters
and, clearly, a profoundly depressed person:

A ZEMERL FOR RABBI NACHMAN

1. Rabbi Nachman Goes into the Woods

He would go, in his broken-heartedness, into the woods
every day, as if he had an appointment
to talk for an hour to God, speaking in Yiddish,
or maybe not speaking, but only repeating one word,

or less than a word, a syllable, a single
vowel, a howl, a pure vocalization,
from which he expected little result. "Zimzum,"
God's apartness, or say, His withdrawal, requires

drastic, desperate measures, and Rabbi Nachman's
keening out in the woods he believed would work
like water that can wear away a stone.

The stone, he said, is the heart—not God's, but his own,
that little by little he might contrive to soften,
to open again, soothed, or even healed.

2. The Rabbi in Town

But in town, what? In Bratslav or Zlatipolia,
surrounded by crowds? What can one do?

                                        Try
to take some comfort: a single person's prayers
God may reject; but in *shul,* in a *minyan,* bound up
with the prayers and the hearts of the others, surely, the Lord
will hear your supplication.
                                        And when that idea

fails to comfort?
                              Then, as the Rebbe said,
"One can dance such a small and delicate dance
that no one can see. And also one can scream
in a still, small voice, making a great scream
that no one else can hear, without a sound,
a scream in the silence, a scream your mind imagines
that penetrates your being. And all being."

3. Equity

Knowing how bad he feels, how much he grieves,
how sharply aware he is of the separation
between himself and God (all knowledge starts
from this), he extorts from this terrible absence
a consolation, extrapolating, to think
how it has to be, at the other end, much worse
for God, who must also grieve cut off from him.

4. Mirrors

The face of the moon reflects the sun's bright light;
so a disciple's face must receive and mirror
the enlightenment of his master, for it is written
in Scripture how the Lord spoke "Face to Face."[2]

And the master beholds himself in his pupil's face:
Imagine two mirrors in opposition
with their infinite repetitions of one another . . .
But this, Rabbi Nachman said, only partly in jest,
would be displeasing to heaven. "If God were content
to worship Himself, what need would He have of us?"

5. The Telling of Stories

Science? It comes from the forehead of the snake.
And Reason? The Rebbe called it an imperfection:

2. Deuteronomy 5:4.

For a man to be whole, he must learn to let go, be simple,
and in his descent ascend to faith and joy.

These are subversive ideas that evil men
seize upon and misuse. Therefore, he contrived
a way to reveal his teachings while keeping them hidden—
in stories. Here he could fashion a garbing of wisdom
to trick the unwary. And good for good men, too.
To waken the sleeping spirit, one must go slowly.
Think how it is when a blind man is healed: they give him
a blindfold; they have to protect him from too much light
that could ruin his sight.
                                    In this he had changed his mind.
A younger man, he had fought against fantasy's dangers,
its snares and delusions distractions from truth and faith,
but this, too, is a power that comes from God.

The struggle is not against the imagination
but within its extravagant realm, in its heights and depths.

6. The Tale of the Man Deep in Debt

The money itself is the least of it. (Still, the amount
you owe is more than you have or can ever hope for.)
It's the shame that oppresses, the fact that you're forced to admit
you're a failure, a fool, have been weighed and found wanting.
    Poor,
you are, as the world reckons, of no account,
a zero, worthless, of negative worth, an abject
object of scorn and derision your neighbors point to,
warning their sons not to grow up to be like you.

Of that shame, he was connoisseur; of that utter dejection
he was the master. In stories a man tells
are the snares his heart has thrashed in, and Rabbi Nachman's
woe is here in its richness.
                                    "And then what happens?"
is the question we learned as little children to ask.

The rabbi tells us how the poor man at last
is brought in his shame and terror into the office
where the rich money lender to whom he owes more than his all
sits and hears him out as he stammers excuses,
lame, unpersuasive, even to his own ears
as he mouths the bitter words.
                                    But the terrible judgment
does not come. Instead, the man waves his hand,
explains he has millions, and says that he doesn't care.
The debt is trivial, nothing to worry about,
and the poor debtor feels both relieved and insulted.
The rich man, seeing this, as an act of kindness
suggests, "There is a way you might work off
the debt, for others owe me sizable sums.
If you will go to my other debtors, remind them
their payments are overdue, and try to collect,
you will bring me hundreds of times what you owe. Agreed?"

Of course.
                    It's the *rebbe,* the man who owes—not money
but a moral debt. And the money lender is God,
Blessed be He. And this is how, with his defects,
Nachman presumes to preach and teach, to remind
us others how much we owe, and to whom, and how
we ought perhaps to consider some partial payment.

Grief is not a disease like pneumonia or diphtheria, and, therefore, what doctors call the "curative" paradigm may not be appropriate. If grief is a kind of pain, the palliative model, which some of the health care professionals are beginning to acknowledge, is the humane and reasonable and essential alternative, inasmuch as it requires that they ask each patient who he is and what he wants and what is acceptable to him.

Depression is a disease, or dis-ease, but even there, one has to tread cautiously. Many of those people who have written about their experience of depression say what I have also found to be true, that the onset of an episode of the disease presents itself as though a veil were being torn from one's eyes and the truth of the human condition was only now revealing itself. Emily Dickinson's description of the feeling is as good as any I know:

> I felt a Funeral, in my Brain,
> And Mourners to and fro
> Kept treading—treading—till it seemed
> That Sense was breaking through—

My daughter—a psychiatrist—is impatient with me for what she considers my perverse reluctance to seek treatment except in moments of particular crisis. She knows that there are medications that would diminish my discomfort, which is reasonable for a daughter to want, and also to help me to function better. But that formulation raises the question as to what my function is. It may be to bear witness as well as I can to the timbres and tonalities of my experience, grim as that sometimes seems.

She also tells me that her object in therapy of people who have been traumatized one way or another is not to get them back to where they were before the assault or the loss or whatever it was, but to proceed as they do in rehabilitative medicine to try to work out the optimal accommodation of each patient as he or she is now, acknowledging and respecting the fact that this is not the same person as before. As the Chinese fishmonger would say, "What can I do for you today, Mr. Bereaved Person?"

The question that occurs to me is how, after that year of distinction, the mourner feels when he is reduced to ordinariness and no longer receives in the exchanges of daily life that honorific suffix.

INDEX

David R. Slavitt is the author of eighteen collections of poetry, twenty-eight novels, and twenty-eight volumes of translations from Latin, Greek, Hebrew, French, Spanish, and Portuguese, the most recent of these being his English version of Joachim du Bellay's *The Regrets*. His *Change of Address: Poems, New and Selected* was published this year. He has taught at Columbia, Princeton, Penn, and Bennington. He lives in Cambridge, Massachusetts.